THE **GRACE** *OF* **FORGIVENESS**

Published by Clear Faith Publishing, LLC
22 Lafayette Road
Princeton, NJ 08540

Cover and Interior Design by Doug Cordes

The interior is typeset in Brother 1816 and Alda.

ISBN: 978-1-940414-19-5

THE **GRACE** OF **FORGIVENESS**

MARGARET BLACKIE

clear faith
PUBLISHING

CONTENTS

ACKNOWLEDGEMENTS

When I began framing this project in early 2015 I had no idea of the journey which was ahead. As the active part of my work towards this book comes to an end, I sincerely hope that reading this book will prove helpful to those who are battling with forgiveness and apology. Nonetheless, it is only as the final version of the book emerges that I begin to recognize how much I needed to write this book for my own process. Without doubt the most surprising aspect of this project has been that over the duration I have reconciled with several people with whom I had long since lost contact but with whom I still felt some awkwardness. These things were not really on my emotional radar when I began. I didn't feel badly enough about any of them to feel that any action was necessary. But there was some residual discomfort. In each case a simple interaction has led to a release of whatever misunderstanding or hurt had been there. More remarkably, I was not the initiator of the contact which has led to reconciliation. In some cases I needed to apologise, in others I needed to forgive. Now, at the end of the writing and editing, I am far more free. And this freedom has opened my being in ways I never considered possible.

There are some personal incidents recounted in this book. Where possible I have omitted the context or changed minor details to preserve the anonymity of those involved. There is one significant exception, the woman whom I call Sr Mary in this book will be clearly identifiable to those who knew me at that time of my life. For those few who know the real person I ask for your generosity on her behalf. Do not let my story taint your own memories. She is also the good woman that you may remember. To anyone else, grant her the peace of anonymity. She has read this manuscript and has been gracious about its publication.

Along the way there have been a significant number of people who have contributed substantially to this project and to the life journey which has allowed this book to emerge. I would like to express my gratitude:

To those who walked with me as I processed my journey over the years: Elsabe O'Leary, Nan Martin, Alice Keenleyside, Dermot Preston SJ, Annemarie Paulin-Campbell, Rob Marsh SJ, Ruth Holgate, Caroline Blackie and Kate Bowes.

To those who read early versions of the book and provided helpful feedback and encouragement: Sarah Broscombe, Andrea Lotz and Juanita Bezuidenhout.

To Esther de Waal for a conversation in Cape Town followed by a few days spent on a writing retreat under her guidance. This got me over the energy barrier to actually begin.

To Biddy Greene for delicious coffee, for encouragement, for the willingness to challenge me and, of course, for the painstaking editing of this book.

To Jim Knipper of ClearFaith Publishing who has been willing to risk supporting the publication of this book. And his great team of editors, proof-readers and designers who have made such a beautiful book out of my humble manuscript.

To the person named Peter herein for inadvertently giving me the key I needed to unlock access to the grace of forgiveness.

There is also a small group of people who have come alongside me, in a manner obliquely related to this project, which has impacted my way of being in the world: Ivan Mann, John Bacsa, Katrina Marshall, Carolyn Meztler and Alli Stillwell.

I'd like to dedicate my efforts here to the people who journey with those who have been wounded. In particular, I'd like to remember my spiritual director who has walked with me these last seven years. In her loving presence I have explored and excavated and slowly, slowly, slowly found my way to both forgiveness and freedom. Through the grace of God and with her support, I have been able to reclaim a painful part of my own history. I can now see that this is a pearl of great price.

Cape Town
Reconciliation Day
16 December 2016

INTRODUCTION

We live in a world where forgiveness is not something we think about much. Certainly forgiveness didn't really cross my radar very often until I was in my mid-thirties. It is not a common topic of conversation until something exceptional happens. For example, in 2006, the Amish community of Nickel Mines, Pennsylvania, gained huge attention. The initial media frenzy was precipitated by the tragic shooting of ten schoolchildren by Charlie Roberts, who committed suicide on the scene. But the story captured popular attention when members of the same Amish community reached out to the widow of the killer within hours of the tragedy. The unequivocal message from the community was one of forgiveness. Their actions supported their words; they set up a charitable fund for the family of the shooter.

In our world, forgiveness of any sort is not often discussed. Until I stumbled into my own forgiveness journey, it very rarely came up in my conversations. Even now, with the exception of interactions with one of my sisters, the topic of forgiveness hardly ever emerges. I am a regular churchgoer, but even in that context, forgiveness is not often high on the agenda in the preaching.

It seems to me that the world we live in is becoming increasingly divided. Or perhaps the divisions that were always there are coming into sharper focus. Either way, in today's world—post-Brexit and after the election of Donald Trump as President of the United States—we are in desperate need of ways to sustain real community. In *The Different Drum*, M. Scott Peck claims that real community emerges only after conflict. If this is true, and I suspect it is, then we need a method for dealing with hurts, misunderstandings, and genuine wounding. A major element of this is forgiveness.

I do not try, in this book, to deal with communal conflicts; my focus is on individual hurts. Why? Because we need to start practicing somewhere! And this is perhaps both the most acute and the most obvious place to begin.

When we read about forgiveness, the examples provided are usually the big ones. Nelson Mandela is perhaps the most obvious icon: a young, radical firebrand went into prison; twenty-seven years later he emerged with a message of reconciliation, even to the point of inviting one of the prison guards to his inauguration as President of the country. Another South African example is that of Linda Biehl, whose daughter Amy Biehl was murdered in Cape Town. Linda and her husband, Peter, forgave their daughter's murderers. Today Linda works with Easy Nofemela, one of the murderers, in the Amy Biehl Foundation. Northern Ireland has the example of Gordon Wilson, whose daughter Marie was killed when a bomb went off at a Remembrance Day service in 1987. He said soon afterward, "I have lost my daughter, but I bear no ill will, I bear no grudge... Dirty talk is not going to bring her back to life."[1] Gordon became a well-known peace campaigner.

The list goes on and on. It includes stories of people who have found the capacity to forgive those who have commit-

---

1   Think RE!, Book 2, Eds Michael Brewer, Ruth Mantin, Peter Smith and Cavan Wood Heinemann, 2005, p83,

ted egregious harm either to themselves or to members of their families.

But what about the smaller stuff? The everyday stuff? The thoughtless act which causes another's emotional distress? Many of these smaller offenses we brush off relatively easily. For the most part, we are able to give the offenders the benefit of the doubt. We know them well enough to recognize that they were just having a bad day and the negative interaction was an anomaly. We quickly forget the offense and move on. The relationship isn't really affected at all.

Occasionally, though, one of those offenses will knock us for a six. We are blindsided and are left wounded and sometimes even profoundly confused. *How could this person whom I have trusted act in such a terrible way?* When such a wounding happens, most of us react in one of two ways.

The obvious reaction is to strike back: *You hurt me, so now I am going to show you.* Pretty quickly, the initial wounding escalates into an all-out fire fight. And the relationship fairly quickly implodes. Here we get to be self-righteous in the end: *I see what she was really like all along. I truly am better out of the relationship.*

The second response, which is perhaps slightly less common but not really any better, is to pull out of the relationship—to simply let the relationship cool to that of a non-functional, amicable acquaintance. It isn't ugly, but again, we get to take the high road: *"I didn't strike back."* Often the person who has created the offense isn't even aware that there was a problem.

There is a popular saying: "Fool me once, shame on you. Fool me twice, shame on me." Both of the above responses play directly into that saying. *If you manage to hurt me once, well that's on you, but I really shouldn't give you a second chance.*

The problem with these reactions is that the first strike isn't usually intentional. When you are dealing with any kind of sustained relationship that has been founded on mutual trust, the likelihood of that person out of the blue, without provocation, intentionally causing you harm is actually very small. People may be thoughtless or selfish and so act in ways that are hurtful. But there aren't that many people who are just mean in the absence of perceived provocation.

I stumbled onto that lesson the hard way. Completely unintentionally, I deeply hurt someone I cared about a great deal— I'll call him "Peter." In retrospect, I can see that I was more than a little self-absorbed at the time, so I was thoughtless and certainly could have chosen a better way of handling the situation. Peter was so broken in the aftermath of the interaction that he had a psychological breakdown. I'd had no intention of causing him pain, and no idea that my words could precipitate such a result. For a while, I was genuinely concerned that he might harm himself.

Most of the wounding we cause does not have such dramatic consequences. But this incident, bad though it was, served a very useful purpose for me. It broke open the importance of considering intent. For the first time, I recognized that, in his view, Peter was fully justified in blaming me for his breakdown. That was his truth. Our one conversation on that particular evening had shattered his world. Certainly, if I'd had any inkling beforehand of the effects of my actions, I would have chosen a different approach. I'd known he would be surprised by the conversation and feared he might be hurt by it. But it was not my intent, at all, to wound him in the way that I did.

As the horror of what my actions had precipitated plagued my mind, I stumbled onto the concept that exposed the doorway to forgiveness for me: the first strike is usually not intentional.

It is worthwhile mulling that thought for a time. What if the first hurt you perceived was not actually intended to cause you harm? Does that change your perspective at all?

Certainly that idea got me thinking about a significant wounding which I myself had suffered.

As I perceived the story for many years, two people were

responsible for shattering my self-confidence on the cusp of my eighteenth birthday. I held them responsible for the full extent of the damage they had caused. It never occurred to me that their intent might have been far less sinister. The metaphorical ankle tap that they had administered was intended to trip me; it wasn't intended to leave me crippled.

The ankle tap was perhaps unnecessary and unkind, but those two people were not responsible for the entire extent of the damage. They could not possibly have known that their actions would feed directly into what I call a fault line in my psyche—an area of extreme vulnerability.

Nearly twenty years after that event, recognizing the separation between the knowledge of what I had experienced and the reality of their intent was the beginning of my pathway to forgiveness. I began to see them as the flawed human beings that they were rather than as the monsters I had created in my mind. And with that, I could begin to see why they might have made the decision that they did. After that it was, for me, a matter of praying for the grace of forgiveness and waiting for it to take hold.

In learning to forgive these two people, I began to grow conscious of other woundings which needed attention: some older and some much more recent. As I have journeyed on, I have come to see that a perception I have carried around for much of my adult life—that forgiveness didn't play a major role in my life—was absolutely true, but not for the right reasons.

Forgiveness didn't play a major role in my life not because I had nothing to forgive, but because I lived by "fool me once." No one got a chance to hurt me significantly more than once; I simply gently withdrew from relationships that no longer felt safe, so forgiveness never seemed necessary.

On further reflection, I realized that I am also very poor at admitting my own mistakes. I am poor at apologizing. So I had never really known what it is to be forgiven.

As you read this book, it will become apparent (fairly quickly) that one of the most fruitful places to begin in the forgiveness journey is to consider the possible intent of the other. The fact that I am in significant pain as a result of someone's action does not mean that person intended to cause me so much pain. It is this invitation to see events through the eyes of another that can provide the key to unlocking the desire to forgive. In her book, *Rising Strong*, Brené Brown writes of the importance of considering that everyone might actually be doing the best that he or she can.

There will be invitations throughout this book to consider the possible position of another. If you are the one who inadvertently hurt the other, can you take on board the reality (to them) of the pain that you have caused?

The experience of forgiving the two people I mentioned earlier had a significant impact on me. For a start, I learned what it means to forgive. I discovered that, for me, the hallmark of forgiveness is the slackening of the emotional tag. I recognized that I had finally managed to forgive when I saw a picture of one of them on Facebook. It was a beautiful picture; the woman looked relaxed and happy. My immediate response was to feel glad that she looked so well. In that moment, I realized I had forgiven her. Up until then, every time I thought about the situation, it would trigger my memory. The thought would set off a painful response; there was still a strong, unconscious emotional link in my mind. This is what we colloquially refer to as "baggage."

Until that point, any situation that subconsciously reminded me of that particular incident would be flooded with the emotional baggage of that wounding. With forgiveness, the emotional tag slackened. I can now encounter similar situations without the baggage. I no longer have any need or desire to avoid thinking about that particular situation. That space, an area I had mentally tried to wall off to protect my vulnerability, is now openly accessible and no longer so sensitive. I have reclaimed that part of my interior world. I have greater interior freedom.

Possessing that interior freedom also means that I no longer unconsciously bring that baggage into new situations. I am able to deal with a new wounding for what it is. This gives greater freedom to my whole way of being in the world and my interaction with others.

The process of engaging as fully as I am capable with forgiveness has had a significant impact on every aspect of my life. I am less fearful of conflict; I am more willing to accept my mistakes; I am more able to own the hurts that I experience. The overall result is that I am far more able to cope with the daily stresses of life. I am more awake to my everyday experience. I am more peaceful, more joyful, and more grateful.

And opportunities to reconcile with people I had long since written out of my life have emerged.

All of this brings me to my desire to spread the word about forgiveness. In conversation with a wide variety of people, I have discovered that most of us struggle with forgiveness. Forgiving is not an easy thing to do because it forces us into a space of vulnerability and requires the greatest honesty we can muster—no matter which side of the forgiving bridge we may be on. I wonder what impact it would have on our world if we all engaged with forgiveness just a little more.

This book begins with a detailed account of why forgiveness is important. I explain the Fourfold Path, which has been used to very good effect by Archbishop Desmond Tutu and his daughter, Mpho Andrea Tutu-Van Firth. As with any psycho-spiritual process, there are a myriad of different possible "methods" one can use. The Fourfold Path is probably one of the simplest. I then describe my own journey, followed by a discussion of some processes involved in coming to forgiveness. Next, we get to the challenges: the areas where many of us seem to stumble, and the reasons why forgiveness is usually not as simple a process as following a formula. Finally, I address the idea of reconciliation. Reconciliation is not a goal of forgiveness, but reconciliation is truly impossible in the absence of forgiveness.

Before we begin, there are several important points that I'd like to address in greater detail.

It is impossible to gain interior freedom in the absence of forgiveness. Those incidents in which we cling to our role as wounded victim and cast others in the role of villain take up space in our being—space that we need in order to live out of the best version of ourselves. In the absence of forgiveness, unforgiveness will rear its ugly head again and again. It will continue to be the baggage we carry into new interactions, and it will continue to define relationships that resonate with similar dynamics. We will never be able to free ourselves of playing out the same roles in the same scenarios over and over again. Unforgiveness is toxic, whether we are aware of its poison or not.

Forgiveness and reconciliation are connected, but distinct. Reconciliation will always require forgiveness, but the opposite is not true. In cases where the person who has wounded us is incapable of recognizing the wounding, reconciliation will not be possible, and it may be that walking away from the relationship is the healthiest option.

Hurts that seem small but continue to plague us are just as important in learning to forgive as the big ones. Anything that remains as a smarting presence in our psyches for more than a couple of months needs attention. Most of the time, with small hurts, the real issue lies within us, rather than in the hurtful intent of the other. Failure to attend to the small hurts means that we are likely to keep stumbling over the same issues. This will slowly erode a relationship. When we face the issues head on, we can begin to see the patterns in our actions and reactions—and identify our own vulnerabilities. If we are open about our struggles, the persons with whom we are in relationship can begin to help us to see what our trigger points are, and we will then be more able to face them in all circumstances with greater grace!

The biggest challenge around small woundings is that they require admission of vulnerability. If we are to continue in relationship with the person who has wounded us, we need to talk with that person about what has happened. This requires courage. To help with this, I have introduced three roles into the book: the one who needs to forgive, the one who needs to be forgiven, and the "forgiveness companion."

The first two roles need no further explanation except to say that as you read the book, you may find yourself thinking about various incidents in which you have taken on one or another of these roles. The forgiveness companion is a third person who is unrelated to the incident at hand—someone who is trustworthy and who will not talk to anyone else about what you share. The role is discussed in greater detail throughout the book, but it is essentially someone who can hold your hand through the process while you are learning to forgive.

For now, as we launch into the book, you will need all the honesty and humility that you can muster. Honesty, to be able to cut through your familiar reasoning and get to a deeper sense of what is actually happening within you. Humility, because you need to be open to the possibility that the way that you have presumed things were may not be the whole picture. You need to be willing to let go of the story you have told yourself about the incident with which you are struggling.

It's not an easy journey, but it is well worth it.

If you are the one who is trying to forgive, then, before you go any further, you may want to give some thought to finding a forgiveness companion. Is there some person who is slightly removed from the situation uppermost on your mind, someone you can open up to, someone who will be able to walk with you on this journey?

2

WHY BOTHER WITH FORGIVENESS?

Why bother with forgiveness? Why is it a big deal at all? Surely, isn't it easier and simpler just to get on with life by gently cutting out those people who cause conflict?

We are living in an era which George Monbiot calls "the age of loneliness."[2] He paints a rather bleak picture of twenty-first century Britain—a picture applicable across much of the western world:

> Yes, factories have closed, people travel by car instead of buses, use YouTube rather than cinema. But these shifts alone fail to explain the speed of our social collapse. These structural changes have been accompanied by a life-denying ideology, which enforces and celebrates our social isolation. The war of every man against every man—competition and individualism in other words—is the

---

2   George Monbiot, "Falling Apart," *The Guardian*, 14 October 2014, http://www.monbiot.com/2014/10/14/falling-apart.

> religion of our time, justified by a mythology of
> lone rangers, sole traders, self-starters, self-made
> men and women, going it alone.[3]

In such a world, under the influence of this mindset, there is surely no space for those who drag us down; those who cause us harm; those who have shown themselves not to be trustworthy. They are to be cut out of our lives with speed and precision, and there is no turning back.

But every time we do so, we shrink the world that we live in.

I certainly have had the experience of choosing to withdraw from a particular relationship for good reason, and have then found myself avoiding a shopping center I knew the other person frequented—and felt increased vigilance when visiting the neighborhood they lived in. I was not moving freely in those spaces. I was constraining myself in my choice to cut this person out of my life.

Furthermore, while I had exiled the person from my life physically—in that I no longer had any physical contact with him—I was not free of his continued presence in my mental and emotional life. With this person in particular, I felt a distinct sense of dis-ease every time I had to go to meetings on the campus where he worked. When I discovered that he had left the university, my sense of relief was palpable.

But it isn't just the physical restrictions that are problematic. The mental constriction is far more difficult. What it is to be fully alive as a human is, at least in part, to be at peace with our past. To be free of any no-go areas in our minds. To be able to explore and own what has happened, and to incorporate that in our future. This is interior freedom.

Human beings are profoundly social creatures. We need connection. There is growing research showing that loneli-

---

3   Ibid.

ness and social isolation are a greater health risk than obesity. There is also increasing evidence to suggest that, rather than anything else, the main issue in addiction is a lack of connection to other people.

In a world that prizes autonomy over quality of relationship, there is no need to speak of forgiveness. In fact, someone who chooses to forgive is sometimes seen as being a bit of a loser. But if we are social creatures who crave connection above all else, then forgiveness becomes imperative. If we are to have meaningful relationships in which we can be truly vulnerable, it is almost inevitable that unintentional hurt will happen sooner or later. So, how do we recover?

The obvious answer is through forgiveness.

But I suspect you may not be convinced yet. After all, who can't afford to shed a few connections? Surely it's better to cut the toxicity out of our lives than to continue on! This is absolutely true, but only if the connection is truly toxic. Reconciliation may not be a wise choice, and ultimately walking away from a relationship may in fact be the best solution for both parties. I certainly have a couple of those clearly terminated relationships sitting in my history. But forgiveness is always important.

Michael S. Barry, author of *The Forgiveness Project: The Startling Discovery of How to Overcome Cancer, Find Health, and Achieve Peace*, writes:

> The stress of unforgiveness negatively affects the immune system. Forgiveness, on the other hand, has an immediate, wholesome effect and long-term benefit in strengthening the immune system and positively affecting the healing process.[4]

---

4   Michael S. Barry, *The Forgiveness Project: The Startling Discovery of How to Overcome Cancer, Find Health, and Achieve Peace* (Grand Rapids, MI: Kregel Publications,2010), p.14.

Barry goes on to supply substantial anecdotal support for his claim. At the center where he works as pastoral counsellor, the Forgiveness Project is a part of the therapeutic package provided to cancer patients. Those patients who have managed to forgive tend to do better with respect to long-term prognosis. (This is not to suggest in any way whatsoever that a patient who does succumb to cancer must have been holding onto some deep-seated grudge!) Nonetheless, people who practice forgiveness have lower risks of cancer, heart disease, and high blood pressure.

In his book *Loneliness: Human Nature and the Need for Social Connection*, John Cacioppo points out that the region of the brain that is activated when we experience rejection—the dorsal anterior cingulate cortex—is also the region which registers the emotional response to physical pain.[5] When we have injured ourselves, we tend to try to protect ourselves from further injury. Oftentimes the self-protective response long outlasts any real danger of reinjury. In the same way, we develop an aversion to the possibility of rejection. Perhaps this is because the same part of the brain is triggered.

Most of us do not make it through childhood entirely unscathed emotionally. We are left with subconscious memories of wounds of rejection. When this tangle of emotion is triggered, we tend to overreact. The fear and perception of the need for self-protection may far exceed the detail of the incident that triggered this response. But the extent of our response can be diminished by learning to deal with new woundings. By far the best way to begin to diminish the fear response is by engaging in forgiveness.

A person who has had a traumatic experience with a dog as a young child can slowly learn that not all dogs are a threat—by approaching dogs in a relatively safe, controlled

---

5   John T. Cacioppo and William Patrick, *Loneliness: Human Nature and the Need for Social Connection* (New York: W. W. Norton & Co, 2008), pp. 3–19.

environment. In a similar way, we can learn how to distinguish between the people who are truly, intentionally hurtful and those who have been hurtful by accident.

If we don't eventually learn to untie the emotional tags, we will always be at the mercy of our subconscious experiences. And we will inevitably be required to sever connections—connections that might have been significant to our well-being. The more we sever connections, the greater our degree of loneliness.

Johann Hari claims that the sensory experience of social connection, deeply woven into who we are, helps regulate our physiological and emotional equilibrium.[6] The experience of loneliness activates an emotional response that makes us less able to accurately interpret social cues. It leaves us more vulnerable to stressors and less able to carry out self-care. This, in turn, leaves us feeling increasingly insecure and more likely to view merely neutral acts as aggression.

As we smart from the pain of initial rejection, we can find ourselves quickly spiralling into a negative feedback loop where we experience more and more rejection. The resulting interior paradigm of loneliness will have a negative impact on both our physiological and emotional sense of well-being—and thus on the attitudes of others toward us.

Of course, the passage of time does help us recover our internal equilibrium. Human beings are remarkably resilient. The problem, though, is that the emotional tag, which may become well buried, does not go away. The next time we are triggered in a similar fashion, we will again have an exaggerated response. The only way to begin to normalize our response to such triggers is to disarm the emotional tag. The most effective way to do this is through forgiveness.

If we fail to deal with these incidents and untangle the

---

6   Johann Hari, *Chasing the Scream: The First and Last Days of the War on Drugs* (London: Bloomsbury Circus, 2015).

emotional knots, we are left with an interior world riddled with landmines. Any interaction with another person can set off one of these interior mines, leaving us wounded once again. Not quite understanding what happened, the other person can be totally confused by the strength of our response to a minor infraction. These landmines will continue to plague us, undermining every new relationship to a greater or lesser degree. And slowly, slowly, the toxicity spreads, not only through our own lives but into the lives of those we are trying to relate to. The only option is to disarm the landmines—slowly sifting through those incidents in our past that require forgiveness.

There is much talk at the moment about "trigger" responses. The current popular conversation is around the desire to limit triggering incidents. While this can be seen as a good, it is virtually impossible to predict how an individual will react to a particular stimulus. For example, many years ago I directed a retreat in which we used sculpture as a way into prayer. There was a large replica of Michelangelo's Pietà in the garden of the retreat house, so we included a meditation on this statue. One woman had a strong reaction—her husband had died about a year earlier and the meditation tipped her back into a wave of grief. We had intended to evoke emotion, but, not knowing her story, we couldn't have predicted the response. On the other hand, three others in the group mentioned this particular meditation as being the highlight of their retreat. Should we have eliminated it beforehand just because it might have caused someone pain? That would have been the logical outcome of the attempt to minimize triggering negative responses.

I believe that it is the responsibility of each of us to try to defuse as many of our own internal triggers as we can. We will probably never fully disarm them, but to be able to get to a place where they are manageable is a reasonable goal. If we do this, we will know when we need to remove ourselves—either mentally or physically—from a situation and give ourselves a bit of breathing space. Pema Chödrön speaks of these moments as being "shenpa" moments—moments of being "hooked," when we feel a tensing, a sense of closing down, moments when:

> we feel a sense of withdrawing, not wanting to be where we are. That's the hooked quality. That tight feeling has the power to hook us into self-denigration, blame, anger, jealousy and other emotions, which lead to words and actions that end up poisoning us.[7]

If we recognize when we are hooked, we can pause for long enough to avoid hitting back at the person who has—probably inadvertently—triggered the response.

Our reluctance to apologize can result in a similar narrowing of our world. Things that we know we have done wrong and have not apologized for—or at least attempted to make amends for—likewise wear on us. These unresolved incidents can leave us feeling defensive and fearful. When we are not able to face our own weaknesses and failings, we will try to escape, to avoid any kind of vulnerability. And the avoidance of vulnerability will leave us profoundly lonely, even if we are surrounded by a network of relationships.

Most of us lead lives that are complex webs of relationships. We are hardly ever clearly victim or clearly perpetrator, and we move between those roles in different contexts without blinking an eyelid. Most of us are far less willing to acknowledge extenuating circumstances for those who have hurt us than for ourselves. We are happy to give ourselves

---

7   Pema Chödrön, "How We Get Hooked and How We Get Unhooked," *Lion's Roar*, February 19, 2017, http://www.lionsroar.com/how-we-get-hooked-shenpa-and-how-we-get-unhooked.

the pass of "having a bad day" when we hurt another, but we will not always accept that as an excuse from the person who has hurt us.

This book is an invitation to hold those two threads together—sometimes you will need to examine those times when you have been hurt, and sometimes you will need to consider the times when you have hurt another. The reason for this approach is to level the playing field a little. In so doing, you'll learn to recognize the passes you are giving yourself , at the same time, giving the other the full weight of responsibility.

It is worthwhile stating clearly at this stage that we humans are emotionally complex creatures. Experiences which affect me deeply may have very little impact on you. The idea of someone "overreacting" is a common complaint. But we have to recognize that the external detail of an incident is almost never a good indicator of its emotional impact. There are many factors that can play into the depth at which we feel a wounding.

Human experiences do not exist on a single spectrum. An experience that is genuinely traumatic is not just a very bad experience. It is an experience that fundamentally rewires the brain. Certain situations—smells, sights, memories—can trigger neuronal circuits which cause a negative physiological response. This response is widely varied, but it is essentially an anxiety cascade—a response to the original trauma. There is no clear correlation between the objective "magnitude" of an incident and the presence or absence of a trauma response.

In a similar manner, there is a difference between those incidents that are hurtful but that we manage to shake off and those incidents that result in a break in a relationship. This latter is the emotional equivalent of a traumatic event. If someone has been triggered in a way that induces a trauma response, then forgiveness will, sooner or later, need to be explored. Whether the result was intended or not is irrelevant. Such a traumatic incident will shape, at a subconscious level, the ways in which we interact with the one who has caused us harm. The result can have clear physiological effects, too: where we had previously felt comfortable in the person's presence, we now find ourselves displaying signs of anxiety—tensed muscles, a guarded approach, increased sweating, a feeling of nausea, and so on.

For the one who has been wounded, there is a clear Before and After. The experiences, which we need to really gird our loins to forgive, are those incidents that are emotionally traumatic—those that cause a rewiring of our neuronal pathways, so that we have a different instinctual response when we encounter the person concerned. There is a clear Before and After. It shapes who we are.

Again, the objective "magnitude" of the incident is irrelevant. If this response has been precipitated, it will need time and an active engagement with the grace of forgiveness to shift. If you are the one who has been wounded, you need to take time to delve into what has happened and discover why you reacted the way you did. *(See Chapter 4.)*

If you are the one who has done the wounding, it is important to understand the significance of what has happened for the other person. If you don't really understand but try to fake empathy, the other person may experience further isolation—perhaps even precipitating a further breakdown in the relationship. Comparison with physical trauma will make the point clearer: when someone has had a near-death experience as a result of a car crash, for example, trying to connect with that person by talking about your own fender-bender will result in a sense of greater isolation, not a better connection. You are demonstrating not only that you have not understood the severity of what he or she went through, but also that you are not capable of appreciating that trauma is not just "a very bad experience." It is something that can be life-altering.

The focus of this book is on events that may seem to

others to be objectively minor but that have precipitated an emotional trauma response. It is worthwhile spending a few minutes considering which events in your life might fall into this category.

There is another significant reason why forgiveness is important. If you listen to any of the spiritual leaders of our time, they all speak of forgiveness. If we desire interior freedom, we must let go of the past. And letting of the past doesn't mean trying to forget about it—that doesn't work; we will keep tripping over it. No, we need to look directly at what has happened, accept it, and then let it go. Doing that is precisely what it means to forgive. Wayne Dyer put it even more clearly, saying that we cannot hold onto any resentment.[8] Again, the only way to let go of resentment is to forgive.

Before you go any further, take a few moments to think about any resentments you are carrying. What are they? Are you ready to begin the process of letting them go?

---

8   "Why We Forgive," *Dr Wayne W Dyer*, accessed March 14, 2017, http://www.drwaynedyer.com/blog/why-we-forgive.

3

HOW DO WE
GO ABOUT FORGIVING?

It is impossible to write such a chapter—indeed write about anything—without talking about the subject in a linear manner. The problem with writing about the process of forgiveness is that it is very easy to get discouraged when you think you have passed through a particular stage, only to find yourself mired in its depths once again. As with the stages of grief, the process of forgiveness can be seen as a spiral.

The five stages of grief are well documented, but most books on grief mention only very briefly that there is not a direct route through those stages, that you will find yourself meandering between anger, denial, bargaining, depression, and acceptance, in no apparent sequence. You can briefly visit a stage much further along the path, but you have only truly reached that particular stage when it becomes your default or resting position. You may catch a glimpse of acceptance when you are still in the anger stage. It can come as a relief, but it is a temporary respite.

Likewise with forgiveness: as the journey proceeds, you may find yourself needing to revisit stages that you thought you had completed. As you journey on, it is a part of the process that you will be able to view the incident that has caused you pain from different angles and in different lights. This may alter your perception of what you earlier took to be true, and so a revisiting of some ground may be necessary.

The major distinction between the process of forgiveness and that of grieving is that in forgiveness there is a clear end. You will know once you have finally and fully forgiven. There will be a shift in interior freedom. The emotional tag will eventually fall slack. But in a grieving process, the tag may never fully go away—and I'm not sure that you would want it to.

It is probably helpful to mention that in many instances, forgiveness itself begins with a kind of grieving. Brené Brown covers this in *Rising Strong*. It may be necessary to grieve the loss of what might have been, or indeed the loss of the image of relationship we once had. In order to forgive, we sometimes have to let something die.

There are many variations on the process of forgiveness. I've chosen to borrow the Fourfold Path described by Desmond and Mpho Tutu in their book *The Book of Forgiving*.[9] I've selected this process for two reasons. First, it gives the fewest steps—which makes it easy to remember where one is in the process. More importantly, Desmond Tutu brings credibility. His daughter, Mpho, co-author on this volume, uses a story of her own to illustrate the journey in a powerful way. The combination provides a book that packs a fair punch!

The Fourfold Path comprises:

- telling the story
- naming the hurt
- granting forgiveness
- renewing or releasing the relationship.

---

9   Desmond M. Tutu and Mpho A. Tutu, *The Book of Forgiving: The Fourfold Path for Healing Ourselves and Our World* (San Francisco: Harper One, 2014).

In most of the examples used in forgiveness texts, there is a clear and unequivocal "right" and "wrong." In *The Book of Forgiving*, the text is woven around the experience of the murder of a domestic worker named Angela, who was employed by Mpho Tutu. Angela was killed in Mpho's home. In such a circumstance, it was clear that harm had been caused. The man who murdered Angela may not have been aware that she actually died, but he would have known that he at least caused her grievous injury. There is no equivocation here; the pain is a matter of public record. Police reports were filed and evidence gathered. The fact of the wrongness of the incident is indisputable.

In the case of smaller interpersonal hurts, this may not be the case. Particularly if there is no physical injury—which must be true in the vast majority of cases—it is entirely possible that the other person may be unaware that he or she has caused any harm. In most such cases, the "facts" of the matter can be pliable and are heavily reliant on perspective. It is helpful to keep in mind the image shown in the illustration.[10]

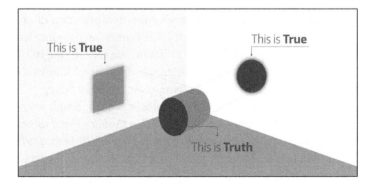

---

10 http://9gag.com/gag/a4YnVGp/please-consider-this-before-talking-and-or-typing

Your own perspective may not be the whole truth of what happened. There are likely to be many factors that influence the way in which you view a particular incident. Forgiveness requires a willingness to accept that there may be another perspective. Perhaps more than one.

The other person will also have a perception of what happened. Neither perception may be completely accurate, as the image indicates. The truth of the shape is more complex than either party is capable of seeing, but if you are each really able to listen to the other, you may be able to get closer to the truth. At the very least, you will each begin to understand that there may be another way of viewing the same incident.

In this book you will find that I give specific instructions to three different groups: the one who was wounded, the one who has done the wounding, and the forgiveness companion. In part this is to help everyone involved to remember that "the truth" lies somewhere in between the different perceptions of those involved.

FOR THE ONE WHO HAS BEEN WOUNDED...

Engaging on the journey of forgiveness requires two characteristics: humility and honesty. Neither is easily come by in the smarting pain of a recent affront. We tend to begin in a space of intense self-righteousness, which precludes both humility and the kind of reflection required by honesty.

If you are still in the self-righteous phase, begin by simply praying for the desire to forgive. If you are still in the blame-and-anger cycle, that's okay. You may need to swim around a little in the shallows of telling your story a few times, in order to allow the anger and hurt to pass through you.

At this stage, a little bit of wisdom goes a long way in terms of whom you choose to share the story with. When you are still in the angry phase, you will quite probably want to create pain for the other person. One of the easiest ways to do that is to bad-mouth him or her. You know the stories people tell: "And then she did this ... and then I said to her ... and then she ... etc., etc." And the response you are seeking is one of outrage and empathy: *"How could she?!!"*

The problem with engaging in that kind of "storytelling," particularly in a smallish community, is that you can't take it back. What you have said will alter the way in which people view the other, and if the person you are talking to is prone to gossip, then the story will spread far and wide, way beyond your control. Your goal at this stage may well be to cause harm to the other, and you probably will. But be very careful. The hurt, which you are presuming was fully intended and consciously deployed may not have been like that at all. Considering that you rarely have the full truth of what happened, such behavior is really unfair and can be profoundly destructive.

This is not to say, "Do not vent." Expressing your anger, frustration, and hurt is important. But find safe spaces to do it in. Most importantly, talk only to people who are outside of the particular situation and who are known to be discreet. Find the support that you need, yes, but if at all possible, find it in a manner likely to be least detrimental to the person who has upset you.

FOR THE ONE WHO DID THE WOUNDING...

If you are the one who has caused some hurt, you may likewise find it difficult to perceive the truth of the other person's perspective. It is quite possible that the hurt experienced by the other is of a much greater magnitude than you anticipated. It may be that you had absolutely no intention of causing any hurt, or it may be that you knew that your actions might cause some pain. The point here is that the response was far greater than you imagined.

The important first step here is simply to recognize that, whatever your intent, their experience is real. The most common response when someone says "You hurt me" is a defensive pose. You will want to claim your innocence and lack of malice. Unfortunately, in the process of trying to defend yourself, you can make the whole situation significantly worse.

In your self-justification, you can end up by creating further hurt for the person who is already wounded. And if the pain you have caused was as a result of lashing out following some minor infraction by the other party, your own desire to be recognized as the wounded party may be an unconscious driver.

The only useful initial response when someone says "You have hurt me" is to ask the offended party to explain what you did and why it hurt him or her. Don't defend yourself. It is highly likely in such cases—where the experience of the wounding far outweighs the detail of what is going on—that some earlier baggage is in play. But it will not be helpful at all to make that suggestion at this stage. Just ask your questions and let the person respond. By allowing the person to express his or her pain, and by simply apologizing for the impact of your actions, you can facilitate that person's ability to take the story further.

Again, humility and honesty are vital ingredients. Here, the humility is the acknowledgement and admission that your actions have caused another person harm. It is painful to the ego to make such an admission, and your ego will try to make excuses for your behavior in much the same way as a child will say "But he started it..." This is why honesty is the second vital ingredient; dare to allow yourself to admit what you truly intended. Allow yourself to step into the shoes of the other. Would you have found your actions troubling or hurtful? Were your actions truly neutral, or did you actually intend some kind of "lesson"?

I am well aware that the suggestions I have made so far may look a lot like a process of reconciliation. You may be presuming that I intend for these things to occur in conversation. That is not necessarily the case. For the one who is trying to forgive, the start of the process begins in reflection. For the one has caused harm, the starting point may require the one who has been harmed to talk about the pain.

Most of the stories of forgiveness given as examples in books on forgiveness are the "big" issues—murder, rape, manslaughter; these issues are all matters of public record, and it is clear that there has been harm done. In the smaller, tit-for-tat kinds of issues that most of us encounter in our daily lives, it may not be so clear that any harm was done. The only exterior evidence of the existence of a problem may be a slight cooling in a relationship.

FOR THE FORGIVENESS COMPANION...

There is a third role you can play in a forgiveness journey, and that is as compassionate friend or forgiveness companion. Your job here is not to get the one who has been hurt on to the next stage. Rather, your job is to help elicit the necessary humility and honesty. It is important to understand that you are not there to mediate. You are simply there to help the person find his or her own way to forgiveness.

To this end there are several crucial elements. First, don't start trashing the person who caused the harm. This will diminish the ability of the one who has been hurt to let the incident go.

Second, don't break confidence on any element of what is shared with you. Your job is to provide a safe space for the one who is struggling with forgiveness. That space will be safe only if you keep the story to yourself.

It is also crucial that you do not try to intervene or mediate in any way. You cannot mediate in a situation where you have a clear allegiance to the one who has been wounded. If formal mediation is required at any point, it will be necessary to involve a person who is truly neutral. Do not try and have a "quiet word" with the person who has done the wounding. Your job is to support the one who was wounded in finding a way to an authentic response.

FOR EVERYONE...

Forgiveness is a grace.

It is vitally important before we go any further for me to state clearly and unequivocally that I do not believe that we can forgive through willpower. I believe that forgiveness is a grace. We can open ourselves to the possibility of forgiveness, but we cannot get there on our own.

Part of the process of opening ourselves to the possibility of forgiveness is going through the steps described above, but the actual interior shift is not something we can achieve on our own. It is a grace, something that blooms in us when we are willing to sit with open hands.

Again: there is a distinct Before and After. If you are not sure whether you have forgiven, then you aren't there yet. That's not a problem; don't let it trouble you. You just have to keep asking for the grace, and keep "doing your work." There is no other choice.

If this is your first foray into forgiveness, you may be looking at months, or even years, before you can let go fully. It may certainly be that you need several attempts. Forgiving is not something you can do for yourself and by yourself; it is a process you need to surrender into. It requires your best efforts in honesty and humility; it is unlikely to be a single pass through.

As you embark on this journey, you need to notice where you are internally—whether you really are ready to forgive. Even if you're still angry and still feel the need to make yourself seen and heard, you can continue to ask for the grace to *desire* to forgive.

On the apology end: it takes grace, too, to truly apologize. Give yourself time and space to absorb that you have actually caused the other person harm. We'll deal with apology in greater detail later, but, for the moment, know that it is okay if you need to take some time to be ready to apologize. If the desire is to reconstruct the relationship, it is better to take your time and to do things sincerely. If you aren't quite there yet, pray for the desire to apologize in freedom. It is not easy to accept that you have wounded another person and to hold yourself accountable for what has happened.

4

INTERLUDE: MY OWN STORY

At this point in the book, we are going to have an interlude. This chapter is the story of my own journey into forgiveness. I'll refer back to it in later chapters, but reading the story as a whole is not necessary to your engagement with the rest of the book. I've included it here because I think it will be helpful to those grappling with similar issues.

Let me begin by saying unequivocally that I do not find forgiveness easy. I'm not sure anyone does, but it has proved to be a major stumbling block for me for most of my adult life.

I'm going to begin by describing the incident that has both been my undoing and my redemption. I do so not to blame but simply to say I suffered for far, far longer than was necessary under the burden of an incident that in itself can be viewed as being almost trivial. But in the intervening twenty-two years (more than half my life!) I have learned much about forgiveness.

I would like to acknowledge my deep gratitude to a woman who, for far too many years, I held as a villain in my life story. I would also like to underline here that while

I didn't recognize this for many years, there is no way that those involved could possibly have predicted the outcome for me. It was precipitated by an intentional, conscious decision to make a point; the resounding impact it would have in my life was not at all evident on the surface.

I am painfully aware that the incident, as described, was a relatively minor one. When it ranks against some of the things others have had to overcome, it is very small. There is no way I should have taken as long as I did to be able, finally, to let go of it. I would go so far as to say that it is almost laughable that it did take so very long. And yet, perhaps that is part of the power of the story. It really doesn't matter what the incident is that trips you up. If it holds emotional baggage for you, then trying to rationalize it away doesn't work. Trying to minimize it or shake it off simply has no effect. It requires an untangling of the emotional knots.

SO ... MY STORY...

The incident took place in 1993. I was head girl of my high school. At the school prize-giving, a shield was always presented to the head girl, and occasionally to both the head girl and her deputy. That year it was simply not awarded. It was a conscious, considered decision made by the headmistress and the deputy headmistress, to indicate their displeasure at my poor communication with them during the course of year. It is worth mentioning that this perceived lack on my part had never been communicated to me!

This is the incident that has plagued me all these years. Some people might think that the issue was trivial. So what was the big deal?

Bear in mind that this was a Roman Catholic girls' school. Passive aggression reigned supreme—as it does in so many good Christian organizations! This was the equivalent of a huge slap in the face. The headmistress—let's call her

"Sister Mary"—and her deputy knew exactly what it meant. Making it all the more pointed was that it was not awarded at a ceremony at which my father was the guest speaker! Several staff members, who had been aware of the decision that had been made, had raised their objections prior to the event—to no avail.

Of course, none of this was really about the shield. It was my total bewilderment. Until the morning of the ceremony, I had been under the impression that I had done a good job as head girl. Nothing spectacular, but I had gotten the job done. I had no idea that there had been any criticism of me or, indeed, as became clear in the days following, of my lack of communication with Sr. Mary.

One can see how my "punishment" would have been painful, and the way in which it was done was far from ideal; but holding onto this hurt for twenty-two years—really?? That's a bit much, surely! Even talking about such an event a year after the fact, with school safely left in the dust of the past, would seem a bit odd.

There must be more to the story. And indeed there is.

For more than a decade, I thought the story had begun at the prize-giving. Now I recognize that in fact it began just after Christmas in 1992—a year earlier. One of my friends, Mandy, who had been appointed as the new sports captain, was killed in a car accident. She was very well liked; one of the school's brightest shining stars—a cool kid who was also kind and thoughtful.

In retrospect, I am horrified that there was simply no real acknowledgement that grief was likely to be a problem for our whole class. There was a funeral during the school holidays, and then, in the first week of term, we had a memorial service, and that was it. Done and dusted. If any other support was put in place, I certainly don't remember it. And my own parents made no suggestion that there might be anything to work through. Looking back, it is clear now that we were all grieving tremendously, but it was under the surface. We didn't even talk to one another about how we were feeling.

That year my friendship circle changed significantly. I think this was in part because I felt awkward being head girl. Most of my closest friends were prefects, and I now had the task of leading them. I remember an incident where one of these friends lied to me about going to some event because she knew I would object. When I confronted her, she was unapologetic. Things like this served to cement my own sense of isolation.

I also recognize, now, that when I am struggling, I withdraw. That is part of who I am. To the outside observer, I appear to be well in control and confident, even when I am finding things tough. I am an articulate and fairly compelling public speaker. I can hold attention. At school, I was a good all-rounder—proficient at academics, a participant in several team sports, and a flutist in various bands and quartets. But I am highly introverted. While I have learned, as an adult, the importance of talking about what is going on internally, in 1993 that understanding was still about five years away. I can remember moments of feeling isolated, but I quickly dismissed them. All this is by way of saying that I am absolutely convinced that no one realized that I had any difficulties. I would have appeared to be coping swimmingly well. I'm not sure that I even knew myself that I was not okay.

So, from Sr. Mary's point of view, the action of not giving the award would have been seen as minor slap down to a kid who appeared a little overconfident and was unaware of her own failings. Framed in that way, I can see how such a decision could have been made.

Now, hopefully, the significance of the story begins to make more sense. What I viewed as a public humiliation was in fact also the focal point for all the unprocessed emotion that had been building in the school for a year as a result of

Mandy's death. That raises the stakes a little, but twenty-two years still seems like an awfully long time.

So what else was going on? I have come recognize in recent years that I have what I call a fault line. It is a direct result of my own childhood. I am the last of five children. It is well established that all children develop coping strategies. My coping strategy was perhaps a little more extreme than most, and I still struggle with it almost daily. Very early on, I began to hide my emotions. As I understand it now, I learned that to express any kind of emotional need created more difficulties than it was worth. This happened to the extent that I grew to be almost entirely unaware of my own emotions.[11] In the typologies of infant survival mechanisms I adopted the "invisible child" strategy.

I remember clearly as a twelve-year-old, in the first year after we had moved to another city, frequently going to bed at about 5 p.m. My family sat down to supper together every evening, but I would eat a bowl of cereal and miss supper. Although I was not consciously aware of it at the time, on reflection I think this was a tough year for all of us and my response was to remove myself. No one was particularly concerned. I think I probably appeared to be slightly better adjusted than my elder sister. I was making friends, doing well at school, playing a sport and apparently having fun. So I missed a few family dinners; it wasn't a big deal. My parents were doing the best they could, and I appeared to be fine.

Alas, over the years, what cemented firmly in my brain was that any emotional need was highly problematic. Added to which, we were fairly strapped financially, so asking for anything above and beyond the ordinary scope of daily life was also problematic. All of this translated into what I now articulate as a profound fear of being a burden on anyone

---

11 It took me several years of intentional effort to train myself to pay attention to how I feel, to begin to learn how to experience emotion.

else. For many years, I articulated this as a fear of taking up space in another person's life. To this day, in situations where I know I am going to have to ask for assistance of any kind—particularly from someone close to me—I literally sweat (a lot!). I have learned over the years that pushing through my fear to express my emotion (in a very small number of safe relationships) is worth the effort. But it remains very costly. In addition, when I start struggling, I withdraw.

So... when I was made head girl, my unconscious presumption was that my task was to get on and do the best I could. And if I could do that without bothering anyone else, so much the better. For "anyone ", read "anyone in authority;" and for "bother", read "speak to, communicate with, converse with, and so on." It never occurred to me that there was any other way to perform the role. And it certainly never occurred to me that any other way of doing it would be desirable. My job, as I saw it, was to take care of things with as little fuss as possible.

It is perhaps a little clearer, now, that we have a perfect storm. I was performing the role in precisely the way I thought best: putting my head down and getting on with it. Sr. Mary and her deputy thought I was deliberately not communicating, which was true—but not for any of the reasons they might have thought. I was not the cocky young upstart I imagine they perceived. Rather, I was desperately trying to cope and yet was completely unaware of my own struggles. I don't blame anyone for not noticing—I had no idea myself!

The combination of the fact that I thought I was doing a reasonable job—because there had been no communication of displeasure—and the fact that I had done what had been asked of me to the best of my ability and had then been told—in a publicly humiliating way—that it wasn't good enough, was shattering. Everything about myself that I had had confidence in turned out to be problematic. I felt I could no longer trust my own sense of how things were going.

The feedback mechanisms I had been using were clearly not adequate. It was as though a hand grenade had been tossed into my safe space. Up until then, I had believed that if I just withdrew a bit and kept my head down, sooner or later things would come out right. Now, as I sat in the metaphorical dark, biding my time, I was hauled out and accused of failing to do the very thing that I believed I shouldn't be doing. I can see this now; I had no idea of the dynamic at play inside me back then.

For far too many years, until I began to understand the dynamics within myself, I blamed Sr. Mary and her deputy for shattering my self-confidence. My self-image had certainly been shattered, just on the cusp of adulthood. In some ways I did come out fighting, with something to prove, but I was also deeply damaged by the experience.

THE JOURNEY TO UNDERSTANDING THAT I HAD A PROBLEM…

The first time I became aware that I had a problem was sometime near the end of my first year at university. I remember sitting in the dining hall one day and suddenly feeling myself overcome by emotion. Of course, no one around me knew that anything had happened. I excused myself as quickly as I could without invoking the curiosity in my friends, and retired to my room. I spent the next couple of days writing. The emotion receded, and I presumed I had processed it. What I wrote then has long since been lost.

Over the next decade, memories of that prize-giving would emerge seemingly out of nowhere and I would once again try to understand what had happened, and try to forgive. The acuteness of the memory would subside for a while, and then, for no apparent reason, it would be triggered again.

The first actual association I have of my memory of these events being triggered in some way was in 2004 (now ten years after the event). I had been on the staff of a Jesuit retreat house for a year. I was assigned the role of coordinating the team of five who were giving the Spiritual Accompaniment II course. As it happened, we had four new staff members (three of whom were Jesuits) who had not been through our spiritual direction training program. The decision was made that these four people would join the course, as students. At a youthful twenty-eight, I was significantly younger than anyone in the course. Enter into the mix that the only Jesuit teaching this course fell ill halfway through and that the director of the retreat house was in Rome for a meeting. The teaching team managed to hold it together—just barely!

The three Jesuits who had been told they had to participate in the course were not very happy. To the best of my understanding, they felt somewhat affronted. A few days after the course had ended, the Jesuit provincial arrived for Visitation. The director (himself a Jesuit) suggested I should meet with the provincial too. In that meeting I was rebuked strongly. The dissatisfaction of the three Jesuit participants was blamed on me, somehow! I still I don't understand why. But the emotional tag of the incident at school came roaring in like a freight train. Again I was being blamed for causing problems when I was simply doing a tough job, in difficult circumstances, to the best of my ability. And again my judgment had indicated that we had been doing well.

Luckily, a South African spiritual director friend visited a few days later and I was able to talk through it all. I still wasn't fully aware, at this stage, that the emotional baggage of the school incident was at play. My own reaction was one of anger at the injustice of the personal attack. I had sufficient information from other sources to realize that the criticism was not justified, but the emotional hand grenade had gone off nonetheless, and I was left profoundly unsettled. Over the following months the emotional storm subsided.

There was a second occasion, in 2006, when the buried emotions from the prize-giving were actively triggered. I began to realize that there was a deeper process at work. On this occasion, I was well aware that I was overreacting to the circumstances, but I seemed incapable of untangling the mess. It began with my directing a week of guided prayer at a university. Directing one person in particular had been difficult. A few days after returning to my job at the retreat house, I received an email from the chaplain to say that this person was very upset and was publicly criticizing me.

I felt as though I had been punched in the stomach. Again the confusion, the fear, and horror of having failed to pick up on a problem, and then being criticised behind my back, came with an explosion of twelve years of unprocessed emotional baggage. This time though, I made the connection. I realized that I was overreacting to what had happened and that my emotional response was not due only to this particular incident. I began to perceive the resonances of the high school experience. Through some careful supervision, I managed to distinguish where I had gone wrong in directing this person from my own emotional baggage. As it happened, a week or so later I went on my own eight-day retreat.

THE JOURNEY TOWARD HEALING...

Almost inevitably, I spent most of the retreat trawling through my memories of the high school experience, trying to untangle some of the emotional knots.

On the fifth day of the retreat, I went to the chapel to pray, just before for my meeting with the retreat director. Much to my surprise, I found myself almost immediately caught up in an imaginative prayer experience. What follows here is what I wrote in my prayer journal.

> I just had the most spectacular prayer period. I began with offering my desire for joy and for love to God who was gazing at me with love and

patience. I had a real sense that the gift was not going to be given soon, that part of my recognition of the preciousness of the gift was that I would have to wait for it. As I stood before God I became aware of Alice, Rob, Ruth and Kate[12] standing behind me, willing you to give me this gift. Then Maggie and Mary[13] joined them. Suddenly I found myself kneeling at the front of an old choir style church. Alice, Rob, Ruth, Kate, Maggie, Mary, sœur Anne, Dermot, Vernon Heinsz,[14] the whole family and all those who have been angels to me were seated in the left choir. While all those to whom I have been an angel were seated on the right. The whole place was filled with people. I lay prostrate before you asking for the gift of joy, feeling the power of all these saints willing me on. Then I found myself getting up and embracing each one. As I embraced each person they gave me a white arum lily. In the end my arms were filled with flowers and I placed them before you, giving back these symbols of what I had received. I was taken aback by the beauty represented by my life. And I heard your reassurance that the gift of joy will come as

12 Alice Keenleyside, my spiritual director; Rob Marsh, SJ, friend and colleague at Loyola Hall who had supervised me after the week of guided prayer; Ruth Holgate and Kate Goodrich, my closest friends at the time.

13 Maggie LeRoy and Mary Fahey. They had done the internship program at Loyola Hall in 2003; we bonded at a week of guided prayer in Frodsham, in Cheshire.

14 Sœur Anne, of the Sisters of St Andrew, held me together during a very difficult period when my father had been interned in Zimbabwe when I was living in France; Dermot Preston, SJ, led me through the Spiritual Exercises and continues to be a spiritual support; Vernon Heinsz, SJ, directed my first six-week retreat in daily life at St George's in Harare in 1997.

> surely as the dawn, but in its own good time. And
> I find myself content to wait, but still desiring the
> gift, perhaps more acutely because I have felt the
> desire of others that I should have this gift.

The real gift of that prayer period was that it was the chink in the much bigger issue of how I saw myself. I recognized for the first time in my life that I had real value, not simply in what I was able to achieve, but in my relationships with others. I had always considered myself a loner and felt that my primary value lay in my intellectual contributions. I was an introvert who chose invisibility as a coping strategy, so my discovering that relationships were central was a totally new idea. And even more mind-blowing to me was that there were a significant number of people who valued relationship with me. This was a watershed experience. It remains one of the most significant prayer periods of my life.

But I hadn't figured all of that out before I went to my appointment with my retreat director. She was not my regular spiritual director so knew almost nothing of my background. She had listened to four days of my trawling through my high school experience and the connection with the recent week of guided prayer, and she thought that this retreat was about healing those wounds. Almost as soon as I had finished describing the prayer experience I had just had, she asked me where Sr. Mary and her deputy were in that picture. As soon as she asked the question, I felt my precious prayer experience shatter. She pushed me further, saying that I probably wouldn't find joy until I had discovered where they fit in. She completely failed to recognize that my prayer experience had nothing to do with the two people who had wounded me at school. It was about something far deeper. I left that room feeling as though I had been violated.

The beautiful, precious image that had spoken into the

much, much deeper issue of my assumed role of invisibility had vanished. I hobbled off to Mass, and when it was over, I cornered my own spiritual director, Alice. That evening she helped me reclaim the experience, and in time I came to see its significance in recrafting my self-understanding.

Nonetheless, it was clear that there was still unfinished business with regard to what had happened at school.

PHASE 1...

About a year later, in 2007, I reconnected with a few school friends and it got me thinking about all these issues. At this point I finally realized that the grief over Mandy's death might have played a role in the life of the school when I was head girl. Up until that point I hadn't understood that we had all been left high and dry. It was also around this time that I began to see the ways in which my childhood had shaped me.

1993

Knowledge is dangerous.
I am beginning to understand
the extent of the paralysis
caused by events of the past.
I think I have finally identified the ghosts.
I recognise the web of sin
that has trapped my body and soul.
I know that in such recognition
lies my redemption.
But memories stir
and a gamut of emotion is evoked.
I know my mind has distorted
the original events, and they

are now frozen in a place beyond truth.
The twisted facts layered over by
years of crippled response.
Who said what to whom
and who did what when
is no longer the key to
disarm the tangled mess.
In the midst of it all
salvation comes in an unlikely guise.
A man, a god, holding it all together,
holding us all together—
in the tortuous silence of unnamed grief.
He was there all along, and none of us knew.
The tangled web of grief and hurt,
of silence and deceit,
bind him more strongly to us
than the nails in the crucifix—
the pain no less agonising.
But there is hope,
there will be redemption.
I am still ensnared
but that consciousness releases power.
The scars will remain
but the paralysis is receding.
In the meantime, while movement returns
and the blood flow is restored
the tissue cries out in agony.
Redemption comes
at great cost.

6 April 2007
Cape Town

With the writing of this poem, the first substantial chunk of my emotional baggage was disarmed. I realized that part of my reactivity had to do with a grief that I had never really acknowledged. Importantly, I also recognized that maybe, just maybe, everyone involved had been a bit messed up that year. Maybe part of what happened to me had not been entirely personal. Maybe I was the scapegoat: the person upon whom everyone's dysfunction got dumped; the one who was sacrificed to make the others feel better.

Perhaps the scapegoat metaphor is a little melodramatic; nonetheless, framing it in this way was the first real untangling of at least a part of my emotional knot. For the first time, I could see that Sr. Mary and her deputy were perhaps a little more human than I had thought. Maybe they too had struggled. I suppose also, being a little older, I could now see that adults have unresolved emotional baggage, too!

PHASE 2...

In 2009, the beast reared its ugly head once more. I was part of small group involved in teaching and promoting spirituality. We met regularly, and we occasionally spoke about the sense of community in the group. In late 2009, out of nowhere, the leader of the group objected when I offered to give input. He said he had had several complaints from people, including university professors, saying that they didn't understand what I was teaching.[15] I was totally blindsided. Again, I had thought that I was giving valuable insight. All the feedback I had received was positive. And I am generally considered

---

15   The significance of this is personal. It felt like an attack on both my capacity to teach and my intellectual capacity—where my identity had largely been formed. To put this in context: the greatest affirmation my dad has ever given me was in 2014. He attended a spirituality workshop I was giving, and a few days later, he sent me an email to thank me for my input, and then came the gem: "I learnt something new." For those conversant in the enneagram, I am a 5 personality type: to be is to be wise.

to be a good teacher. Yet no one else in the group expressed surprise or offered a different opinion in that meeting.

I was shattered. Again the emotional baggage exploded— my self-understanding laid to waste; I was really no good at perceiving how people were receiving things. This time it was a full frontal attack, but I hadn't given any input for several months, so the complaints must have been old ones. Again I had been criticized behind my back.

I formally withdrew from the group a few weeks later.

This time, I was fully aware that my reaction was connected deeply with the pool of still-unresolved emotion that was lurking inside me. This time, I had a good spiritual director who was able to walk with me into the morass of emotion. As the journey progressed, the antechamber of school experience gave way to real exploration of the cave of childhood wounding. It was at this point that I began to describe what had happened as the "triggering of a fault line": hitting that particular nerve resulted each time in an internal earthquake. The very ground upon which I had built my self-understanding was being disrupted.

This time, I was able to separate out quite quickly which emotion was associated with the deeper, older wound, and I spent a good amount of time cleaning out the muck. Part of this healing process has been accepting that the fault line will always exist. Nonetheless, another significant bundle of emotional entanglement had been released and separated from the incident at school.

PHASE 3...

Finally, in 2011, I was given the key that was the beginning of real freedom. In a series of incidents on which I simply cannot elaborate,[16] I came to recognize that I had severely

---

16 Elaboration would require telling Peter's story. I cannot do that without causing further pain.

damaged someone whom I cared about a great deal. As I mentioned in the Introduction, the fault line I triggered in Peter resulted in a full mental breakdown.

I am still horrified by what was precipitated, entirely unintentionally, by my actions. Ironically, or perhaps simply through the grace of God, this ended up being the final key to my letting go of the school wounding. In recognizing that my actions could have terrible, unintended consequences, I recognized, for the first time, that the same might be true for others, too.

I realized that, although an emotional earthquake had happened to me in 1993, Sr. Mary and her deputy were not responsible for the full extent of the damage. To put it in physical terms, they had ankle-tapped me, with the intent of making me stumble a little. In fact, not only had I fallen over but the damage to my leg had been sufficient to cripple me.

For nearly two decades I had blamed them for crippling me. In truth, they were only ever accountable for trying to make me stumble. Finally, finally, forgiveness was a possibility. I was beginning to see them as human; no longer did I view them as filled with malicious intent—perhaps, like all of us, just a bit wounded. I went to Confession, both for my part in causing Peter such terrible harm and for having held such anger toward Sr. Mary and her deputy for so long.

I started to pray in earnest for the grace of forgiveness. In 2012, I described some of this in a chapter of a book I was writing on Ignatian spirituality. When *Rooted in Love* was published in 2013, I thought I had forgiven them. I had certainly let go of the blame. Soon after that I managed to get hold of Sr. Mary's email address (the deputy headmistress had died some years before), and I composed a letter which I intended to send her, along with an electronic manuscript of the book. But something held me back. I didn't send the email.

In retrospect, I realize that part of my motivation was to let her know how I had struggled. Much as I hate to admit it, I did want to cause her distress. I was not yet in a place of freedom—although I was definitely moving in the right direction. The emotional knots were gone, but the grace of forgiveness had not yet taken root. I now recognized that I had to let go of the sense of self that I had molded around that particular wounding. It was no longer healthy for me. I would constrain my future growth if I could not let it go. So I continued to pray for the grace of forgiveness—because I desired freedom.

FREEDOM AT LAST...

In October 2014, I stumbled across a picture of Sr. Mary on Facebook. It was a beautiful picture. She looked both relaxed and happy. Much to my surprise and utter delight, I found myself happy that she was happy. Finally, finally the emotional tag had been released. She was no longer the villain in my story.

The grace of forgiveness had taken hold and I had found my emotional freedom.

But we're not quite done...

Four months later, in February 2015, I found myself looking at the letter I had written to Sr. Mary in September 2013 but had never sent. Again I found myself wanting to send it. I copied the text into an email, edited it slightly, and attached an electronic copy of *Rooted in Love*. I sat with the cursor pointed at the Send button. I prayed an Our Father, and halfway through I knew I couldn't send it. I had to go to a meeting, so I stopped. About an hour later, I returned to my computer. I knew I had to make some changes. I removed the electronic copy of the book and edited the letter to remove all mention of the book. I realized that my desire in almost sending the book had been to prove just how much I had been wounded. It was no longer necessary—and it was certainly not kind!

Again I paused to pray an Our Father—then I sent the new email.

The very next morning, after I had finished my prayer time, I looked at my phone—and there was a response! I was profoundly moved by it. Sr. Mary had had no trouble remembering the incident. She was clearly shocked at the impact that her action had had on my life. She asked me for my forgiveness and told me that, fortuitously, they were having a Mass for healing that day, and she would be praying for healing for herself. Most surprisingly, perhaps, she thanked me for telling her what had happened.

I responded immediately, reassuring her that I had indeed forgiven her and that, while she might have cause to regret the initial action (which she said she had indeed regretted many years before), she could not have predicted the effect her actions would have on me. And that I had no doubt that, had she had any inkling, she would have chosen differently.

RECONCILIATION...

In that brief interaction, which took place over a period of fourteen hours, I feel that we have reconciled. I never thought that reconciliation with Sr. Mary would be possible—or even desirable. I presumed that I would want to avoid her for the rest of my life. I know now that if I did have occasion to see her, I would embrace her. I see her no longer as the villain in my story, but as a wounded human being. No more or less wounded than I am.

I am truly astounded by the way in which my soul has been moved, through the grace of God. And I pray fervently that Sr. Mary will not take my story as a burden.

On the same day I heard from Sr. Mary, I received an email from a woman who had been a few years ahead of me in school.[17] I had been blogging about forgiveness—but not

---

17   Kate Bowes.

in direct relation to this incident. This is what she wrote:

> Another comment on the forgiveness post I wanted to make is what it is to be on the receiving end of forgiveness and how miraculous that can be and feel. I am a person who holds such a gift and gets to hold it consciously thanks to the generosity of another. Now it is silvered, beautiful, solid, a treasure; once it was a shattered shard of glass, a piece of a mirror that was untouchable and utterly unapproachable. It is one of the most remarkable things I've ever been a part of.

It was such a gift for me to hear that. It was a confirmation of my own sense of reconciliation—that true reconciliation is possible.

Memories of that prayer experience with the arum lilies and roses[18] have re-emerged. Where my retreat director had tried to force Sr. Mary into the picture, I now, finally, can welcome her in. I want her to stand next to me as I hand out roses to those who have been angels to me. She has been my greatest teacher. I have finally learned not only what it is to forgive but also what it is to be reconciled. I pray that this process will be a gift for her, too.

It amazes me that even this prayer experience, which was nearly destroyed, has been fully redeemed. (I often use this as a cautionary tale when I give spiritual direction courses.) It is more beautiful now than I could have imagined possible. It seems that the grace of forgiveness is not simply a one-way street. It is not only my future that has been freed; my past too has been broken open in a new, and

---

18 The roses were incorporated into the prayer experience when it was recovered as I worked through my memory of it with my spiritual director. Having received the arum lilies, I handed out roses.

unexpected, way. The comment of my friend that the shard of glass has become silvered, precious, to be treasured, gives me hope that this might be true for Sr. Mary too.

IN THE END...

The grace of forgiveness has been hard-won for me. And again, I am aware that the school incident that precipitated this learning was in some senses quite minor, but the emotional minefields that were drawn in because of it have been worth unearthing. It has led me to explore places that I might not otherwise have explored. And in reaching this place of forgiveness, I feel as if I have been redeemed.

Let me add that this not a naïve position. I am well aware that I have, both knowingly and unknowingly, precipitated pain in others. This is not a place of victory, but one of profound humility.

The longer I sit with it, the more I begin to think that the incident at school has in fact been a very great gift to me. If this incident hadn't gotten tagged with the other emotional baggage, I wouldn't have worked so hard at trying to let it go. If the precipitating incident had been more serious, I wouldn't necessarily have been so invested in freeing myself of it. But following the fault line back to its origins, and cleaning the festering wound along the way, has proved to be my liberation. "The stone that the builders rejected has become the cornerstone." This element that I have loathed in myself has become the key that unlocked my self-exploration. How utterly, utterly extraordinary!

5

TELLING YOUR STORY

From the last chapter, it will be evident that the way in which a story gets told changes over time. In some cases it takes a little while for the full impact of the story to emerge. The way I chose to tell my story in the days after it happened is quite different from the way in which I reported in the last chapter. I was truly hurt, angry and confused in those early days. All I could see was a massive, unprovoked attack. I had no idea that a large part of my own response was actually about me and my own stuff, my own experiences.

Remember honesty and humility. Tell the story as you truly perceive it today. The only way to get through the different layers of response is to allow yourself to feel what you feel and find a way to honor those feelings at the same time as releasing them.

There are two distinct elements to telling your story as part of a forgiveness process. The first element is the detail of what actually transpired, and the second element is the impact that the incident has had on you.

Things can happen every day that cause us minor upset and offense. How we deal with these varies from situation to situation and from person to person. In some instances, we are capable of saying clearly: "That was a problem for me," and the other person involved quickly apologizes and we move on. In other instances, we decide to keep quiet and consciously let it pass. In either case, in a matter of days, or even hours, the incident is forgotten.

This kind of incident, which doesn't lodge in your psyche, isn't terribly important. The quality of connection that you have with the other person isn't particularly disrupted. Provided you are able to vary your decision to stay silent or to speak up in appropriate response to the situation, this is simply part of the dynamic of what it is to be engaging in the world. These kind of incidents don't require an active process of forgiveness.

Occasionally, though, you will be pained by something in a way that does penetrate deeply into your being. This kind of pain may fundamentally alter your relationship with the person or people in question. There is a severance of trust. It is not impossible to recover a good and beautiful relationship from this place, but it will not happen without an active process of forgiveness. In such cases, there is a distinct Before and After. This results in a fundamental shift in the relationship. The trust relationship may be recovered, but only through forgiveness and reconciliation. Recovery will never occur if the issue is swept under the rug. Until it is resolved, it will cause one or both of you to trip periodically. And if it is not resolved it may well destroy the relationship.

The confusion and struggle we have with forgiveness is located, in part, in the fact that the incident that we are able to shrug off and the incident that causes us deep pain may not look all that different when viewed from the outside. And different people react in different ways: an incident someone else shrugs off without a second thought may be deeply hurtful to me.

The subjectivity lies in part in the quality of relationship that exists between me and the one causing offense;

it is also influenced by my own journey thus far, including especially any previous wounding. An incident which triggers my interior fault line can cause a substantial hurt to me, regardless of the detail of what happened, and regardless of the intention of the other.

If you genuinely want to embark on a journey of forgiveness, it is useful to have a companion who can travel the distance with you. This "forgiveness companion" must be— or become—a "safe space" in which you can tell your story. You will tell your companion what happened and what your reaction was.

Your companion must—importantly—be able to hold a middle ground in his or her reaction to your story. It is not helpful to have someone belittle your reaction with a "But that wasn't really so bad, was it?" response. Nor is it necessarily beneficial if the companion completely endorses the strength of your response and shares your outrage (especially if it was a rather minor action that triggered your emotional reaction).

This last point needs further explaining. Your journey of forgiveness may ultimately reach a point at which you and the other are prepared to reconcile. Your forgiveness companion must be able to support you even to that end: to the point where you want to put away all the feelings of outrage so that your wound can heal. If your forgiveness companion has participated too much in the outrage, making that final transition may be tricky for both of you.

Your forgiveness companion should, ideally, not have a personal relationship with the person who has wounded you. Even more importantly, your forgiveness companion must be able to keep your story to himself or herself!

If you cannot find a reliable forgiveness companion, a journal can work too. Writing down what has happened can help you find your voice. At the very least, it will help you begin to move into processing what has actually happened—rather than sitting in the repetitive loop of wounded outrage. (Make sure, though, that you keep your journal in a place where others won't stumble across it.)

Tell your story with as much honesty as you can. What was it that transpired? Who was involved? What happened inside you? How did you feel at the time? How do you feel now?

Don't worry at this stage about whether your response seems reasonable, rational or justified. Simply tell the truth about your own experience. Be very careful to be specific about what actions were taken. Don't say "He's such a jerk!"; say "I'm so angry that he did x, y and z." Don't be afraid of expressing your anger, but do take care to express it in places where it can be contained and where it is unlikely to add fuel to the fire.

A word of caution here: take care to own your response! For example, say: "I feel angry, hurt, mad, etc.", rather than: "That made me angry, hurt, upset, etc." Again referring back to my own story: for many years I credited Sr. Mary and her deputy with having destroyed my self-confidence. I now know that they didn't do that to me. And that was not at all their intent. Their actions did precipitate a crushing response in me. But the response was my own, and grappling with that response has taught me a great deal about myself and where my fault line lies. As a result, I can now cope with similar situations without being utterly undone by them. They can still knock me sideways, and it takes me time to right myself, but I know now why I respond to that kind of stimulus in the way that I do.

Owning your response is an essential part of the whole process. It is the first step in moving from victimhood to agency; or perhaps from child to adult. Whatever the action of the other person, your response is yours. It moves you from reaction to response. If you claim that someone has made you angry, then you can justify any action you take against that person—because they started it anyway. This is the reaction of a small child: "But mommy, he started it!" If you claim the anger as your own, then you are acknowledging your responsibility for whatever further action you take. It is a move into emotional adulthood.

That seemingly insignificant syntactic shift from, "You made me angry" to "I am angry" has the potential to change the dynamic in a relationship entirely.

Again, remember honesty and humility. Take time to explore how you feel. Where are you feeling it in your body? Anger tends to reside in upper back and shoulders; anxiety often presents as nausea or pain in the belly; grief and sadness are likely to cause a tightening in the chest and throat. Is your body telling you anything?

At this stage, don't worry about analyzing too much the reason for your reaction; simply allow yourself the time and space to truly own what it is that you feel. If it is possible to talk through your feelings with a forgiveness companion— or some trustworthy person—that will be helpful. But again, be very careful whom you choose. At this stage, it is most useful to have someone who can simply help you to explore how you feel.

It may be beneficial to use art, poetry, or some other creative outlet to express how you are feeling. It may be that you need to turn to the creative outlet first, before you can find the words. The ordering doesn't matter. Just allow yourself to fully honor what it is that you are experiencing.

It may take several attempts before you feel that you have been able to express what is actually going on for you. Take your time until you have a reasonably sharp image of where you are.

Now for some specific advice, depending on the role you are playing in this particular sequence of events.

FOR THE FORGIVENESS COMPANION...

Your role at this point is to help the wounded person tell his or her story. The most effective tool you can use is to listen, and then to repeat back what you think the person is saying.

This will allow the person to "hear" himself or herself. Your primary intent must be to help the person to articulate and understand what has happened and how he or she is feeling.

Do not try to offer any explanation for what the other might have intended. Do not suggest that the person is overreacting. Your only task at this stage is to treat the person with respect and compassion.

If there are things about the story that don't seem to add up, feel free to ask clarifying questions. It is very useful to assist in unearthing the detail of what has happened. The wounded may be tempted to gloss over his or her own negative reactions, making the story harder for you to comprehend. If this is the case, gently point out the areas that seem confusing to you and ask for more detail.

Under no circumstances should you try to approach the one who has done the wounding. In fact, you should not try to speak for the one who is wounded in any way at all. Your role is only to hold a safe space in which the one who is wounded can explore what actually happened.

FOR THE ONE WHO DID THE WOUNDING...

You may be entirely unaware of what is going on at this stage: that something you said or did elicited a negative reaction. If you are aware that there is a problem—that something disruptive has occurred—it is usually helpful to communicate that you are aware of this. If you think you may have caused the problem, then it can be helpful for you to admit that there is an issue, and that you are willing to talk about it. If the one who was wounded asks for time, then it is best—for both of you—to allow the other the time and space needed.

Sometimes there are small incidents that may appear trivial to one person but cause a big problem for another. You may be aware that there is some disruption in the relationship, but you may not recognize that it is you who has somehow caused the problem. When there is a clear disruption to a relationship, it is useful to indicate that you have noticed this. Then ask the person to tell you what they see as having happened.

FOR THE ONE WHO HAS BEEN WOUNDED...

The focus of this chapter has been on how you can begin to tell your story. It is often tempting to gloss over any negative reaction you may have had. Do the best you can to be completely honest about everything that has transpired—while acknowledging the limits of your perspective. And own your own feelings. Do not try to have a conversation about what has happened with the one who has wounded you until you have taken time to recover your equilibrium. Premature contact would very likely exacerbate what is already a bad situation.

6

EXPLORING THE CONTEXT

Once you have a clear image of what you have experienced, you can begin the process of exploring the wider context of what it is that happened. But exploring the wider context is truly useful as part of the forgiveness process only after you have honored yourself. Many of us, when we have been wounded, quickly turn inward to shaming and blaming ourselves for being hurt. The honoring of our own processes is an important antidote to that.

It is true that you may be partly culpable for precipitating the action of the other. But you will only be able to own the part of the process that is genuinely yours once you have taken care of the wound. Imagine the wound to be a crying toddler, and the culpability to be a sulky teenager. You will not be able to give the sulky teenager your undivided attention until the crying toddler has been attended to. Trying to converse with a sulky teenager while the wailing toddler is still tugging on your trouser leg is not going to get you anywhere.

There are four important elements to the exploration of the context. First is awareness of the situation in which both you and the other are operating. Second is consideration of the intent of the other. Third is exploration of internal resonances: Do your feelings remind you of some other situation you have experienced? Fourth is assessing personal resposibility: Is it possible that the person's action was a response to something you did?

Let us look at these elements in more detail.

1. *What is the situation?* Was there anything happening around the time of the incident which was an unusual stressor of some sort? A stressor can be anything that would result in distraction. In the example I used from my own life, the stressor was the death of my schoolmate. But it could be something far less dramatic— illness, depression, new responsibilities, uncertainty over the future—or even just an increased workload. The list really is endless. Is there anything in your environment which could have either heightened your own sensitivity or created a greater degree of thoughtlessness on the part of the other?

2. *What was the intent of the other?* This is an incredibly useful question and one that is important to ask. My own experience of unintentionally wounding another broke open for me the significance of this question. I precipitated tremendous pain completely unintentionally. This made me realize that, in the course of day-to-day interactions between people who are generally good-natured, the first strike is probably not intentional. It may be thoughtless, it may be selfish, but only rarely is it done with intent to cause pain.

3. *What are the internal resonances?* Have you been through a similar experience in the past? When there is a resonance, oftentimes it indicates the presence of a fault line—a deep wounding, often

with roots in childhood—that has been triggered. This means that the strength of your response may well be far greater than is reasonable. The person who has hurt you is responsible for the action that triggered the fault line but is not responsible for the entire emotional storm it has precipitated.

4. *Are you partly responsible?* This is a tough one to explore, but it is possible that what you are experiencing is not actually the first blow to be landed in this particular exchange. Did you do anything to cause injury to the other which resulted in this intentionally hurtful response?

The perspective from the "wounded space" is almost always slightly distorted. The idea here is therefore to open yourself to the possibility that there may be other ways of viewing what has happened to you. At this stage, you will not yet be conversing directly with the person who has wounded you, but you are opening yourself to the possibility that there may have been more going on than you initially presumed.

There are two important points introduced here. First, the other person is human and therefore subject to experiencing the same kinds of stresses and strains as you are. Second, your reaction may have something to do with who you are and with your own history—which is above and beyond the action of the other. Both of these aspects are factors mitigating culpability on both sides.

Too often when we are hurt, we quickly strike back, intending to hurt the other as we have been hurt by them. The problem here—and it is a big problem—is that if the action of the other person was unintentional and they are unaware of the impact that it has had, their first sign that there is an issue will be this intentional strike from you. If you can simply sit for long enough with the hurt and pick through the possible contributing factors, and, particularly, if you are able to approach these in conversation, you may be able to stop the "violence" at the first strike. However, once you have retaliated intentionally it is a far uglier and messier process.

It may also be that you are already on the receiving end of an intentional strike back. It may be difficult to ascertain whether this is the case without having a conversation with the person who has hurt you.

This step in the forgiveness process is the pause between action and response. It allows for the possibility that you may not have access to the whole "truth" of what has happened, despite how much you feel the pain of what you have experienced.

I had an experience with a close friend that very nearly ended the friendship. In fact, had it not been for her persistent inquiry about the root of the matter, the friendship probably would have died because I did not realize how much I had shut down. The hurt wasn't that great, but it precipitated a reflexive response in me to withdraw. What had been a safe space no longer felt safe, so I was out of there.

It was only in considering the wider context that I realized what I was doing and what her intention had been. As I explored this interaction, I realized that there had been a breakdown in communication, and I needed to risk being hurt in opting for resolution. Her persistent questioning was vital to my coming to the awareness that I had been freezing her out. In the process, I was forced to recognize that I was not coping well at all with a larger, unrelated situation. My denial of that struggle had laid me open to overreaction. Again it took honesty and humility on my part to admit to myself what was actually going on.

Engaging in the wounded space with this broader perspective only works once you have honored your own process. Pay close attention to your internal dialogue as you engage in this space. It may be very tempting to underplay your sense of wounding. You may find yourself saying things like: "It really wasn't so bad." This is where honesty becomes paramount. If you really were badly hurt, it is important for your own journey that you do not deny that. Stand in the truth of your pain. There may also be a message for you about earlier woundings, which will be helpful to resolve in due course.

The purpose of taking a wider perspective is not to downplay your pain, but, rather, to raise the humanity of the other. What you are looking for here is a realization—perhaps slow-growing—that the other is not an evil villain out to get you but, in fact, a normal, bumbling human being whose inadvertent mistake has caused you some degree of pain.

Pause for a moment and consider how often you excuse yourself for poor behavior because you were feeling overwhelmed or threatened or angry or insecure, or even just exhausted. Is it not possible that the other person was also having an "off" day? For women: don't underestimate the role of pre-menstrual tension. (Although be very cautious of leaping to this conclusion on behalf of the other person!)

There is a slight caution here: if someone persistently treats you badly, that is probably who they are. Don't try to find excuses for persistent behaviors. When you are being verbally or physically abused by someone, this is part the how they reflexively work out their own frustrations or woundedness—but you don't have to be the punching bag! The focus in this chapter is the once-off blindside from someone who usually treats you with respect.

WHAT DO I MEAN BY FAULT LINES?

As I've explained above, "fault line" is the name I have given to my own woundedness. I have at least one very sensitive area that always precipitates an internal earthquake when it is triggered. I can now recognize when this is happening, but it still takes time for me to recover.

For me the fault line is triggered by any instance in which I come to see that what I think is true and what I am told is going on are not consistent. This calls into question my capacity to observe accurately and to discern—which in turn causes massive self-doubt and a huge amount of self-recrimination of the "I should have known better" variety. I understand the dynamic of my own childhood sufficiently well to realize where this comes from, but it doesn't stop me from falling headlong into the trap every time anyway!

It is tremendously useful to recognize when a fault line has been triggered. It will help you make sense of the emotional earthquake that has just happened. Importantly, it will help you see what pain you can in fairness attribute to the other person and how much is arising from your own emotional baggage. But it is definitely not helpful to go into self-recrimination at this stage. Simply own the part that is properly yours. When you are ready to discuss the situation with the person who has wounded you, it may be helpful to acknowledge to him or her that you can see your own inner reasons for reacting so strongly; nonetheless, you would like to point out the action- which has wounded you.

If you are aiming for reconciliation, fully owning what is properly yours in the interaction is imperative-. You may have a strong tendency toward feeling shame. If this is the case, make sure you confide in someone who will bear witness to your shame and will be able to love you in your vulnerability. This person may be your forgiveness companion. If you don't have a forgiveness companion, speak to a good friend. The only way to combat shame is to bring it to the light, and the way to do that is to share it with someone.[19]

---

19 If shame plays a big role in your life, I strongly recommend reading Brené Brown's *The Gifts of Imperfection: Let Go of Who You Think You're Supposed to Be and Embrace Who You Are* (Center City, Minn.: Hazelden, 2010).

FOR THE FORGIVENESS COMPANION...

The greatest temptation at this point for the one who was wounded will be to underplay what has happened. As the wounded one begins to see the bigger perspective, there may be a real temptation for the person to assume full responsibility for what has transpired. This can send the wounded one down a shame spiral. Phrases like "I shouldn't take things so personally" are indicators of avoidance. The challenge here is to hold in one picture the various perspectives that are coming into view.

The fact that the hurt may not have been intended does not make it hurt any less. A helpful question to ask the wounded one is whether he or she has anything to learn from the experience. Is there something being triggered inside? Is it possible that the one who did the wounding was not at his or her best? Your role is to help the wounded one gain the clearest possible view of the bigger picture *before they begin* a conversation with one who did the wounding.

A word of caution: Pay attention to your own triggers. If you find yourself over-identifying with either party, you may well have work of your own to do.

Avoid the temptation of fabricating stories about what might have been going on. Just stick to what is actually known. Your role is to help the wounded person own his or her truth, and to find the best words to tell their story. This will go a long way to helping the person have a constructive conversation—at the appropriate time—with the one who has done the wounding.

FOR THE ONE WHO HAS BEEN WOUNDED...

Two things are crucial. Can you view the other as a flawed human being? And is it possible that some of your reaction is actually your own emotional baggage? Do not make the mistake of underplaying what has happened. If there is a real issue in the relationship, if trust has been severed, you will need to deal with the problem or walk away from the relationship. Avoidance by talking yourself out of feeling wounded will simply not work in the long run. Finally, are you open to the possibility that this may have been partly precipitated by past actions of your own?

FOR THE ONE WHO DID THE WOUNDING...

If you are aware that you have caused harm to someone else, even if not intentionally, you might need to give the other person space to process whatever s/he needs to. In this case, it will be useful to consider how your actions may have been received. It will also be helpful to examine your own intentions very carefully and honestly. Your ego will try to justify your actions as being fair and uncomplicated. Take time to consider what you truly did intend. Was the sideswipe just an unfortunate consequence of some other action, or was it at least partially intended'

It is very helpful to understand that the wounded person's reaction may not be totally due to your hurtful action. That person may in fact be struggling with some old wounds. Nonetheless, assessing and then taking responsibility for your part in triggering their fault line is still vitally important and necessary.

If, however, your actions were precipitated by something that the other person did, you will have to go through your own process of forgiving them.

The conversation between the two of you will usually begin when the one who was wounded approaches you. However, if this does not happen, and if the relationship is to be restored, sooner or later you, as the offender, might have to begin the conversation. If any kind of functional relationship is to be restored, someone has to make the first move!

7

ENGAGING THE ONE WHO HAS WOUNDED YOU

Once you feel that you have explored the situation for yourself and have managed to separate, in as far as you are able to, the various threads involved—what the other person actually did; what impact that has had on you; what that precipitated in you; and what the other might have intended—ask yourself if you are willing to forgive. That is to say, do you have the desire to forgive?

If you do not, then first pray for the grace to desire to forgive. It's the first step.

If you are already willing to try to forgive, then there are a couple of different routes available to you.

At this stage, if the other person is no longer a part of your life, simply pray for the grace to forgive. Make a practice of praying for that grace at least once a day. Occasionally something will happen to trip the memory of the incident or the person. When the tripping of the memory no longer elicits a negative response from you, you have forgiven.

There is no way of predicting how long this will take—indeed you may find it takes years, or you may find that you are already there. It may be that as you read this, you recognize that you have in fact let go. But don't worry if this hasn't happened yet; it isn't that quick for most of us! And most of us have to consciously choose to forgive. It may also take several different periods of concerted effort!

In my experience, forgiveness is primarily experienced as freedom. The emotional burden has been relieved, or a part of your soul that has been out of bounds is now accessible. Another key indicator is how you feel toward the other person. It is fairly common to want to avoid a person who has harmed you. Once forgiveness has occurred, you are more likely to be able to tolerate their presence. You may not be overly eager to see them, but you will no longer feel it necessary to go out of your way to avoid them. Remember, though, the shifts here toward forgiveness may be incremental. You may experience a degree of increased freedom, which will be sufficient for a while.

Forgiveness within your own heart and mind is highly unlikely to precipitate any change in the person you are forgiving. The aspect that may well change is the way in which you view the person. In forgiving, you no longer need to play the role of "victim" to his or her "villain." This will allow you to drop some of your projection onto that person and will also allow you to notice when he or she acts in ways inconsistent with being a villain! You will be able to see that there is more to this person than you previously thought. For example, you may begin to notice his or her acts of generosity and warmth.

If the other person is a part of your life and you do want to explore the possibility of reconciling the relationship, you will have to have a conversation with him or her regarding what has happened. Make sure you take time to prepare, and remember that the other may not have any idea yet that he or she has caused you any harm. Also be aware that the other's actions may have been a reaction to something that you yourself did.

The conversation will be an invitation to the other to acknowledge what he or she has done and to apologize, but it must be approached with as much freedom and generosity as you can muster. It is entirely possible that the other person will not react well to being "called out." Do not be surprised if the first reaction is one of defensiveness.

Remember: take care of yourself both before and after the conversation. Beforehand, prepare what you would like to say. Make sure that the other person has the time and mental space to hear what you are saying. To this end, it is probably a good idea to make a formal appointment or date to speak with him or her. You want to make sure that you are unlikely to be interrupted and that the person has the mental space to actually hear what you are saying. To just drop the other person into this kind of conversation can end up compounding the problem. After the conversation, you might take some time to journal about your experience, or, if you have a forgiveness companion, perhaps give your companion a call.

It isn't reasonable to expect a full, considered apology within the context of a single conversation. The person may need time to absorb what you have said and to consider what he or she intended. If the other needs time—give it! Don't forget, you yourself are already engaging in a longer, reflective process. I would suggest that you gently encourage the other to take time to consider what you have said and what might have been going on for him or her before offering any real apology. If this seems strange to you, pause for a moment and consider how it might feel to be on the receiving end of such a conversation. What might *you* need in those circumstances?

After the conversation, it is useful to reflect on what has happened. Were you able to speak your truth? Did the other person seem to receive what you shared? Did they offer any further information in terms of their own intentions or the circumstances under which things occurred? Do you feel that you were heard in the conversation?

Did the other person bring up anything that is legitimately yours to apologize for? This question may take a bit of sitting with. If the other person is very defensive he or she may well look for behaviors of yours that have been troubling. So take time to examine your own memory and motives here. Take time to ask for details about what you did that caused the other person's pain. If the answer is not precise, then it is probably just a defensive reaction to being called out.

Again it is important that you take time to honor your own process. It is most probable that you will have to reconsider some of the things that you held to be true in the light of the conversation. Here are some options:

- What had appeared to you to be an attack out of the blue may in fact have been retaliation for some action on your part. If this is the case, you may need to consider offering an apology for your prior action.
- The other person may be incapable of owning his or her culpability. It is important that you are clear on what you feel you need an apology for. Do you need the other to be sorry for the whole emotional storm you have suffered, or simply for a thoughtless action?
- The other person may attack you further. For some people, a display of emotional vulnerability elicits a very defensive response that can feel like a secondary attack on you. If this is the case, it is not likely that further conversation will be helpful to you. You could make it clear that you are open to the possibility of speaking again about these issues sometime in the future, but only if the other can do it in a manner in which he or she does not attack you.

It is important at this stage to consider what you desire for the future of the relationship. Do you desire reconciliation, or do you want to walk away? While your feelings are likely to be one or other of these options, in the real world, it may be that you have no desire to reconcile but that never having to interact with this person again is not a viable option. This can be the case in many professional relationships and in family relationships. Perhaps the most obvious example of this would be in the breakdown of a marriage where there are children. You may long for a world in which you do not have to interact with your ex-spouse, but that person remains the parent of your children and therefore sustainable interaction over the long term is the only available path.

If reconciliation is your goal, it is clear that forgiveness is necessary. True reconciliation will not occur until you have managed to forgive. However, if you are walking away, forgiveness is still strongly advisable. In the absence of forgiveness, the person who hurt you will still take up emotional space in your being. In my experience, forgiveness increases interior freedom, which can break open new vistas of possibility. Forgiving a significant wound may allow for the healing of older woundings that are still catching you out—even though this may be happening unconsciously.

The hardest road to walk after such a conversation is the ambiguous middle one—where neither reconciliation nor walking away is possible. This road is the toughest because the one who has wounded you may not recognize the significance of his or her actions nor the impact that it has had on you. It is likely that the behavior will not change in any way, and therefore, you are vulnerable to further hurt. Once again, most books on forgiveness do not deal with this middle road. Conventional wisdom would say reconciliation and severance are the only real options. Alas, those may not be choices you can make. Nonetheless, forgiveness is still a worthwhile goal.

These three possible paths will be dealt with in more detail in later chapters.

FOR THE ONE WHO HAS BEEN WOUNDED...

Prepare for the conversation with one who has wounded you. Make sure you are clear in your own mind about what it is that you feel needs to be addressed. The one who has wounded you is responsible for causing you hurt, but if a fault line has been triggered, no apology offered will provide sufficient balm to soothe all the pain. If this is the case, you may do well to consider some kind of counseling to help you deal with the prior wounding.

You must also be prepared for the possibility that you may have inadvertently precipitated at least part of the response. If, after the conversation, you feel that you have not been heard but you do want to effect reconciliation in the long term, you might have to consider a mediator. The mediator should not be your forgiveness companion! It should be a person who can provide a safe space for both you and the one who has wounded you.

FOR THE FORGIVENESS COMPANION...

The key here is making sure that the one who was wounded is getting a wider perspective (and therefore a greater sense of the truth) of what actually happened. It is unlikely that the conversation between the two parties will be emotionally neutral. Either it will be helpful or it will precipitate greater damage.

If the wounding incident that was first presented to you by the one who was wounded was in fact precipitated by something that that person did, the person may not find this easy to admit. Your role is to help him or her process the whole story (in as much as it is known at any point along the journey). If you notice that things aren't quite adding up in your mind, it may be helpful to ask some gentle questions around what the other person actually said in the conversation.

FOR THE ONE WHO DID THE WOUNDING...

Hearing that you have wounded someone else is difficult. Whether you intended harm or not, your actions have caused injury. Take time to allow yourself to absorb that. Then consider what your intent actually was. Your first response is likely to be: "But I didn't mean it." It may well be true that you didn't intend harm, but were you in fact selfish or thoughtless in your actions? Take time—as much time as you need—to consider what the other person has said. If he or she was wounded by your actions, it is appropriate and necessary to offer an apology. However, an apology is much more meaningful when you take time to consider your culpability and to own the specific actions for which you are sorry.

Don't worry too much if your response to the initial conversation is defensive. Very few of us are capable of instinctually responding with generosity when we feel that we are being accused of doing something wrong. Take time to reflect. Once the dialogue has been initiated, you can go back at a later date and try to offer a genuine apology. The situation is not hopeless until one party actively shuts the door.

APOLOGY

Offering an apology is a complex process. It is not as simple as merely saying "I'm sorry." It requires us to recognize that, whatever our intention, we have caused harm to the other.

When dealing with the kinds of emotional injuries caused in the passage of everyday life, it is not uncommon to be surprised that one's actions have caused offense. You may have genuinely been trying to do the best you could. In such cases, your first inkling that there is a problem in your relationship with the other may be a cooling off in response to you, or even a direct assertion from the person that he or she has been hurt by you.

The most common response to hearing that we have caused pain is to defend ourselves: "I didn't mean that; therefore you cannot have experienced pain." The problem with this response is that it can really heap coals on the head of the person who is already in pain. Just because the slight was not intended does not mean it has not caused injury. Most of us quickly engage in self-justification: "I really am not such a bad person because..."

In so doing we find every reason under the sun why we should not be held accountable for our actions. We were thoughtless because we were rushed or stressed or concerned about something else. We find every excuse for ourselves, hoping that the person we have wounded will give us a pass and will somehow no longer feel so wounded.

It doesn't work.

Even if you are able to accept that the other was wounded, you may still do everything you can to find excuses for your own behavior. The "apology" might go something like: "I'm sorry, but..."

There is a saying that takes many different forms; my favorite is "Everything before the "but" is bullshit." The "I'm sorry, but..." apology is actually: "I'm not really sorry at all. I'm just saying sorry because I've been brought up well and I know that these words are the appropriate ones in such a situation."

In the normal course of events, when someone comes to you to say that they have been wounded, it may take some time and some serious reflection before a sincere apology is possible.

Apology, like forgiveness, requires honesty and humility.

You will need to acknowledge and accept that, whatever your intention, the other has been wounded. While there are some circumstances in which one's actions have completely unknowingly caused harm, in many cases the one who caused the harm will be aware of the possibility of harm coming from his or her actions. The incident that taught me this was the one I have already mentioned, when I inadvertently precipitated Peter's major depressive event. I knew that what I had to say would probably hurt him, but I had absolutely no idea that the consequences would be so drastic. While I did not intend to hurt him, I knew that my action was likely to cause him some pain. I also dealt with several aspects of that particular interaction very badly. As result of becoming aware of the extent of his wounding, I had to come to terms with my own selfishness. There are several things that I could have done which would have been kinder. These might not have softened the blow but would have been better for the subsequent exchange.

I had to accept that my actions had caused Peter significant trauma. For him there is a clear Before and After, and that particular conversation on that particular night was the precipitating factor. Even if I had dealt better with the extraneous details, it is highly likely that his response would have been the same. My actions hit a fault line in him that neither of us was aware of before that night.

We all need to accept that we may be capable of causing tremendous harm.

AS AN ASIDE...

For the one who has been wounded, there is a task that may help you empathize with the one who has wounded you.

You could spend a bit of time considering the occasions when you have caused others pain. Have your actions been intentional or not? Are there some people whom you have intentionally wounded—either directly with cruel words, or indirectly by retelling stories about them or about your interaction with them?

Take your journal, and give yourself some time to write down a few occasions where you have caused someone else harm. For each occasion, write down the exact circumstances. Consider how your actions may have impacted the other.

How does it feel to recognize that you are capable of hurting someone else?

If you cannot think of anyone, you are probably not being honest with yourself, or you are not sufficiently aware of the impact that you have on others—it is highly unlikely that you would not be able to complete this task.

BACK TO THE APOLOGY

The humility aspect of apologizing is the reining in of the ego—the willingness to embrace your own flawed humanity. All of us have blind spots; all of us have areas where we give ourselves a pass for being self-centered; all of us have areas of our own wounding where we unknowingly transmit pain to others.

Some years ago, I left the UK without telling a friend of mine. The oversight was not intentional; I was just wrapped up in what was going on in my own life. My fear of being a burden on others meant that I didn't arrange for a final meeting. In the process, I really hurt my friend. My own childhood wounding was unintentionally being passed on to another.

It was only recently that I finally apologized to her sincerely. My first apology after she discovered my absence was full of self-justification: the "I'm sorry, but..." type. The second one was simply acknowledging her hurt and saying I had been wrong and that I was sorry. Unsurprisingly, it is the second one that has facilitated our reconciliation!

Another consideration: Is there a particular area in which you always give yourself a "pass" for behaving badly? Is it time to seek healing for the wounding that you yourself carry? Remember that old saying: "Hurt people hurt people"—if you don't commit to a healing journey for yourself, you will unconsciously transmit your pain to others.

Bear in mind that I am presuming here that we all carry a degree of wounding. For some it is greater than for others. For some it manifests as a kind of insecurity: "I am less than the world;" for others it manifests as a kind of feigned confidence: "I am greater than the world." Neither position is good or healthy! And this wounding is the baggage we carry into all our relationships.

True apology is not easy, but, like the outcome of forgiveness, it affords freedom. Even if the other is not able to respond with forgiveness, the act of making a sincere apology frees us from the burden of carrying the incident further. The freedom that comes with true apology does not require an act of forgiveness of the other.

Because true apology requires self-examination and an acknowledgement of what you have actually done, it demands the greatest truth that you can muster. The old saying that the truth will set you free is absolutely spot on. Engagement with the whole truth—or as much of the truth as you can access at the time of the incident—and a public admission of your own culpability will release that space in your soul. *(Note: "public" here may simply be a conversation with the other person involved.)*

Reconciliation is possible only in the presence of true apology and genuine forgiveness. If either of the parties involved have not reached the freedom that ensues from apology and forgiveness, reconciliation in any real sense will not be possible.

One word of caution: be careful about offering an apology in the absence of a clear indication that the other person knows about the offense and has in fact been wounded. Such revelations are often more about unburdening your own guilt rather than genuine concern for the other.

FOR THE ONE WHO HAS BEEN WOUNDED...

If, in the wounding, your fault line has been triggered and you are feeling the pain associated with prior woundings, no apology given by the one who has wounded you on this occasion will feel adequate. They can only apologize sincerely for the triggering event; they are not responsible for your personal history. Again, if a fault line has been triggered, some counseling may well be a good idea. Nonetheless, allowing yourself to forgive this person for his or her action may open up the possibility of forgiving older wounds in yourself.

Whatever the case may be regarding the triggering of a fault line, you need to give yourself time to feel the balm of the apology. Remember that accepting the apology does not require that you commit to reconciliation. Is the apology on its own sufficient, or do you feel that you need some kind of act toward making amends? You may need to wait until you have sorted out the effects of prior woundings from other sources.

FOR THE FORGIVENESS COMPANION...

The key question to hold in the forefront here is whether the apology offered is appropriate to the situation. It may not cover the whole extent of the felt experience if a fault line has been triggered. But is the apology in proportion with the action? Does the apology appear to be sincere? Is there any further action required by the one who has apologized to substantiate the sincerity of the apology?

FOR THE ONE WHO HAS DONE THE WOUNDING...

The sincerity of the apology is crucial. Take responsibility for your own actions. You need to accept that you are capable of causing others harm, even if unintentionally. Ask yourself whether there is anything that you need to learn from this. Maybe this stems from a part of your personality that you didn't notice before. It is helpful to ask for the grace to see things clearly, and for humility.

Now that you have become aware of what you have done this in this situation, it may be helpful to ask yourself whether you have in fact done similar things in other situations. Is it possible that there are other hurts that you now see also require an apology? In addition, you may need to forgive yourself along the way. Here it can be tremendously helpful if you are part of a faith community that offers some kind of reconciliation with God.

It is possible that you may need to make some kind of amends. Is there anything that you could do which would clearly demonstrate the sincerity of your apology?

9

RECONCILIATION

The kinds of slights I am primarily dealing with in this book are the product of breakdowns in relationships that have already been established. They are not, for the most part, acts of random strangers; rather, the pain has been caused by someone who is already a part of your life. The presumption is, therefore, that some kind of reconciliation is desirable.

Reconciliation without true apology and genuine forgiveness is not possible. The process of apologising and forgiving does not happen overnight. I believe that both are a grace: something to be desired, something that we can open ourselves to, but ultimately not something that we can achieve through willpower or good intention.

As a result, real reconciliation of a serious relationship breakdown may take a long time. In the interim, what is required is a clear willingness on both sides to do the work each has to do to afford the apology and the forgiveness. There may also be a need to make amends of some sort, or an undertaking to cease from a particular behavior.

Bear in mind that, for the one wounded, the relationship has changed. As a result, the relationship for both of you has been altered. It will require significant effort from both of you to figure out what the relationship now requires from each of you. It will not be exactly the same as it was before. It will require give and take and a genuine willingness and curiosity about what it means to live in changed circumstances.

Reconciliation is based on the presumption that trust can be reestablished. This is only true if the wounding action was an aberration rather than a habitual pattern. Reconciling when the wounding behavior is part of a habitual pattern is very often a sign of an abusive and co-dependent relationship. Unless active steps are taken, likely with professional help to break the abusive pattern, reconciliation is unlikely to be advisable for the one who was wounded.

In South Africa, it is evident now that, despite the Truth and Reconciliation Commission, insufficient effort was put into figuring out what it meant to actually live as part of the "Rainbow Nation"—either as a previously wounded person or as a person who wounded others. In recent years, racial tensions have escalated. The TRC facilitated apology and forgiveness for apartheid-era crimes, but it seems that little thought was given to helping all people, or groups, to live consciously in the new space. It is not that repeated apology is necessary but, rather, that the systemic distortion of society from decades of living under apartheid remained and continued.

Likewise in relationships, once the apology has been made and the one forgiving is committed to seeking the grace of forgiveness, further excavation of the hurt itself may not be necessary. Both people must however be committed to finding a new equilibrium in the relationship. This means that the one who needed to apologize must recognize that the words of the apology are not sufficient to bring about reconciliation; they must back up their words with appropriate action. Likewise, the one who is seeking to forgive must back up this search with kind action toward the one who has wounded him or her. This new equilibrium may or may not require significant changes.

In the reconciliation of established relationships, there will have been a precipitating incident that has caused the final disruption of relationship. However, it is highly likely that the process of dialogue and reflection between the one who was wounded and the one who did the wounding will uncover earlier incidents that were simply papered over. The process of trying to reconcile may well feel like the opening of a can of worms. If that is the case in your situation, it will probably do both of you well to find a mediator who can facilitate the dialogue, and individual counseling to ascertain what you need to learn as an individual.

It may be necessary to spend considerable time on an iterative process of apology and forgiveness before the real work of reconciliation can begin. This requires huge generosity of spirit from both people involved. It is helpful here to keep in mind Brené Brown's assertion in *Rising Strong* that most people really are doing the best that they can. Can you allow for the possibility that the person involved in this reconciliation project is doing the best he or she can?

The reconciliation process will require a rediscovery of the relationship. In the absence of a willingness from both parties to find a new equilibrium, reconciliation will not be achieved. Furthermore, reconciliation will not occur simply because the desire to reconcile has been expressed. The work of reconciliation must be done. Let me stress again: *this may take a significant amount of time.*

It is probably helpful to revisit the reconciliation project together periodically to check in with one another and to see how each of you is doing. Progress toward reconciliation is unlikely to be linear. There will be setbacks along the way. In addition, new areas of sensitivity on both sides are likely to be revealed. Being willing to be open and vulnerable about your self-discovery will be an important part of the reconciliation.

Bear in mind too, that taking any kind of morally superior stance is the death-knell of reconciliation. You cannot reconcile if one person is standing on the high ground of being "the innocent one." In any long-term, significant relationship, there is no clear victim and no clear oppressor. There are just two wounded human beings trying to love one another. The fact that the other was in error on this occasion is happenstance. It could just as easily have been something that you did that precipitated the disruption in relationship.

Reconciliation will take you both to your wounded places. The decision to commit to reconciliation can bring about healing for both of you—not just for this particular incident but for the woundings that you both carried with you into the relationship.

It is worthwhile to hold onto Pema Chödrön's teachings on "shenpa moments": those moments when you find yourself momentarily internally paralysed by something another person says or does. In those moments, pause! Stop, allow yourself to breathe, and try not to react the way you usually do. Notice what has caught you. Is this really about the intention of the other person, or has something in you been triggered? If it is the latter—and it usually is—take time to explore what that trigger is within yourself.

When you have recovered from the shenpa moment, try to have a conversation with the one with whom you are reconciling. This will help both of you begin to understand one another better and to own what is actually yours, rather than projecting that onto the other.

FOR THE ONE WHO HAS BEEN WOUNDED...

Reconciliation requires living into a new way of relating. It requires a continual commitment to forgiveness. It requires a curiosity about the person with whom you are in relationship. It may be useful to make a new commitment in some formal manner. Marion Woodman speaks of having had four different marriages.[20] She and her husband went through four distinct phases during their fifty-five years of marriage. Each one required a new commitment.

Perhaps most importantly, is there anything you need to change with respect to the way in which you deal with conflict going forward? Reconciliation is not primarily about the other changing; rather, it is about training yourself to let go of the projections that you held regarding this person, to allow more of this individual to be revealed to you.

FOR THE FORGIVENESS COMPANION...

Your services may no longer be required in a formal capacity. Your job is to support the reconciliation. You should not bring up the conflict again in conversation. If the one who was wounded wants to talk about it again, he or she must initiate the conversation with you. If this happens, it is helpful to ask why the person is revisiting this space. It will probably be most helpful to the people involved if you are willing to step back gently and allow them to live their way into the new relationship.

FOR THE ONE WHO DID THE WOUNDING...

It is important here to remember that there is no way to go back to "how it was before." While you may not have felt the relationship shifting, your actions have precipitated a change in the relationship and a new equilibrium must be found. Many of us find accepting the forgiveness of another challenging, precisely because it means that we must accept that we were at fault.

Looking backward: Ask yourself what was going on

---

20   Marion Woodman, "Dancing in the Flames—'Two Marions'," *Awaken*, October 24, 2012, http://www.awaken.com/2012/10/dancing-in-the-flames-two-marions.

inside you that caused you to behave in the way you did. Is there a part of you that is not being seen or heard in the relationship, and how are you going to deal with that?

Looking forward: Are you willing to risk entering a new relationship dynamic with the other? What do you need to take on board in terms of their response and what have you learned about yourself?

10

WALKING AWAY

There are some circumstances in which walking away is really the best option. If you cannot have a conversation without hurting one another and your lives are not too closely intertwined, it may be best to part. Certainly, if the relationship is abusive in any way, walking away may be the wisest choice, and the healthiest one for both parties.

Under most circumstances, the decision to walk away will be precipitated by an attempt to have a conversation about the hurt that has happened. It is possible that the one who has been wounded finds that the one who has caused the wounding is simply unable to accept any responsibility for his or her actions. It is common here for the one who had caused the wounding to inflict further pain. A common strategy to avoid taking responsibility is to blame the one who was wounded for being "weak" or "hypersensitive."

For the one who was wounded, this can be deeply disorienting and painful.

It is also possible for there to be circumstances in which it is the one who has done the wounding who needs to walk away. This is usually the case where the one who is wounded has had a fault line triggered through the incident and is not yet aware of the connection to prior wounding. In such a case, the one who is wounded will require an apology for the whole extent of emotion that they are feeling, even though only small part of that was in fact the fault of the one who caused the wounding. In such a case, no apology can be offered that is deemed sufficient. And the one who was wounded may be unable to let go of the incident.

In such cases it will be clear that, while the one who was wounded is seeking an adequate apology, it is unlikely that he or she will be trying to forgive. The motivation for seeking the apology for the whole emotional quagmire is to situate the blame clearly on the shoulders of the one who caused the wounding. This negative reaction is based on the belief that, by casting the other as "terrible villain" and himself or herself as "innocent victim," the emotional turmoil will be resolved. This simply won't work. Notice, though, that this attitude would require the offender to collude and accept the role in which he or she has been cast. Forgiveness cannot happen in this state of polarisation.

In any circumstance where there is a serious mismatch between the desire for forgiveness and the desire to apologize, it is very difficult to recover the relationship. And under such circumstances, it is worth considering the possibility of simply letting the relationship go, and walking away. Whether that will require a formal declaration or not is dependent on the people involved and the nature of their relationship. In most cases, where there has been a highly emotionally charged incident, it will probably require one person to say "I'm done."

The decision to walk away should not be taken lightly. It may be that a bit of breathing space will help to settle things and a temporary break from communication is warranted rather than a complete and permanent severance. *(See next chapter.)*

It is vital to recognize that the decision to walk away does not let one off the hook of doing the work of apology or forgiveness. If you don't do the work of letting go of this negative interaction, it will follow you. Every time you have an interaction that shares some elements of the situation from which you have walked away, you are very likely to bring all the unresolved baggage into the mix. This will be true whether you were the one who was wounded or the one who caused the wounding.

That baggage may or may not be conscious. Regardless, it will heighten the emotional intensity of subsequent, unrelated situations. Nevertheless, if you truly desire interior freedom, you will, sooner or later, have to do the work of letting go. Perhaps, more practically, failure to do this work is likely to result in significant complications in at least one relationship in the future. If you cannot let go of this incident you will transfer it onto someone else when you get triggered in a similar fashion. You simply cannot escape this reality.

I have certainly had the experience of being crippled by relatively minor incidents because I was carrying the baggage from an earlier wounding and was unaware of this. I was far less able to deal with the minor incidents productively because I was experiencing a much greater depth of wounding than was actually appropriate to the situation.

This consideration may require a little of time, both to mull over and to allow the smarting pain of the current slight to dull a little. The key to determining whether some of your own baggage is influencing your response is to ask yourself whether your reaction is proportional to the slight you have experienced. If you think it is possible that you are overreacting, the chances are that there are incidents from your past that still carry baggage for you, and something inside you has been triggered—so you are bringing a load of unresolved emotion into the situation.

As you consider your own baggage, you may find yourself thinking about incidents that occurred a significant time in the past. It may be that you have not seen the people involved for a very long time and are not likely to see them in the future. Because this is sitting in your past and is highly unlikely to intrude into your future, you may think that it is not necessary to reexamine it. "Let sleeping dogs lie." But again I would caution against simply trying to bury the hurt and hoping it will go away.

A friend of mine speaks of her anger when her sons are asked to participate in fund-raising events for children in Africa. Her rage sits in her own losses as a white Zimbabwean now living in Europe. She has a strong desire simply to close the old chapter and live into her new life. But the old chapter keeps showing up. Only when she has faced into her anger and grief and allowed them to flow through her will she find freedom.

There are numerous Internet memes about closing doors on the past. The problem is that if you have not come to peace, to a place of interior freedom with respect to what has happened, it will never be truly past.

The final reconciliation of my own high school story occurred when someone asked me what had happened— there is a chapter in my book *Rooted in Love* that speaks of the incident without giving detail. As I told him the story, I found myself bored. I didn't want to be telling this tired, old story anymore. I was done. It was at that point that I was at last able to reach out to Sr. Mary and tell her that I had forgiven her. In so doing, I was finally able to let go of the hurt, a release that has undoubtedly created greater interior freedom for me.

It may be helpful to pause for a moment and consider whether there are incidents in your past that you have walked away from but that still return to haunt you. Perhaps it is time to pray for the grace of forgiveness. It may be that you need to forgive another person; it may be that you need to forgive yourself—or both.

Take some time and allow yourself to work through the whole forgiveness process.

There are some occasions where walking away is genuinely appropriate. In such cases, you may choose to revisit the ending of the relationship in your mind. It might help to think, from time to time, about the ending of the relationship—until you feel that you have learned what you needed to and that you are free from the burden of whatever baggage you were carrying.

Perhaps you are the one who has been walked away from. This is more often the case when you are the one who has been hurt. And the person who has hurt you has cut contact. This is always hard to deal with. You will probably feel as if there are issues that you can only resolve in conversation with the other. It is very difficult to accept that the other person has simply cut contact. You will probably be tempted to try to draw them back into conversation somehow. If the cutting of contact comes after a time of attempted engagement, and if you think it possible that the other has made a considered decision, it is best to simply let them go, and find a way to help yourself process whatever is left unresolved (using a journal, a forgiveness companion or some kind of counselor).

If someone cuts you off for no apparent reason and you are unaware that there was a problem, then you are almost certainly the one who has unknowingly caused some harm. In this case you would be wise to try to make contact (possibly with the help of a mediator or mutual friend) in order to begin an honest conversation. This may fail, but it is always a good idea to make the attempt.

Once the relationship has been severed, it may not be possible for you to entirely avoid seeing one another again, especially if you share significant mutual friends. In these circumstances, commit simply to being polite—and charitable. If you have decided to sever the relationship and friends are curious as to why, the wisest course of action is to simply acknowledge that you have fallen out. Don't feel obliged to give any explanation—you can only give your side of the story, and that is unlikely to cast the other in a good light.

In these days of online social networking, it is perhaps important to make sure that you also sever the online connection. Cyberstalking the person who has decided the relationship must end is simply unhealthy. If you share a mutual circle of friends, you probably won't be able to avoid seeing some content related to them; simply pass over it.

FOR THE ONE WHO HAS BEEN WOUNDED...

Under most circumstances, the choice to walk away will be yours to make. It isn't an easy decision. There are several factors to consider: The first is whether a real apology is possible. Second, even with a real apology, are you willing to forgive? Third, even if you do forgive, do you desire to continue in relationship?

If there are ties—such as shared children or business interests— that link you together and necessitate continued negotiation, the complete severance of the relationship will not be possible.

Even if you do decide to terminate the relationship and you have no real ties to that person, you will still need to work toward forgiveness. It is most likely, though, that this will take place after you have chosen to sever the link.

Under these circumstances, it is important to take time to grieve what you have lost.

FOR THE FORGIVENESS COMPANION...

There are two important questions at this stage. First, is a final severance of the relationship actually necessary at this time, or would taking some time apart be a better option? Second, is the one who is wounded carrying related issues that are getting in the way of the resolution of this particular problem? That is to say, is this particular incident part of a larger pattern for the one who was wounded? If so, they probably need to be gently encouraged to do some work on exploring that pattern.

FOR THE ONE WHO DID THE WOUNDING...

It is unusual for the one who has done the wounding to feel that walking away is necessary. The only circumstance under which this is usually a good option is when it is clear that you have hit a major fault line in the other. That person has been crippled by some small action on your part and requires you to take responsibility for the entire flood of emotion that he or she is experiencing. Usually the person wounded in this in such circumstance has no interest in forgiveness or real reconciliation. You are the villain in his or her story, and there is no possibility of reframing. Under these circumstances, there may be real grief for you.

It is far more common for you to be bewildered and shocked by the sudden severance of the relationship. In this case, take time to figure out what you are actually responsible for. It is important for you to take ownership of what you have done—and to do the work of interior apology and forgiving yourself—even if you are unable to express that to the one who was wounded.

TAKING SPACE

It may be that it is impossible for the wounded person and the one who has wounded him or her to get on the same page with respect to apology and forgiveness. A sincere apology offered by one person may not be sufficient for the one who was wounded. If the one who has apologized is unable to offer any further apology, it may be necessary for both parties to take some time to do individual work on the incident. There are a couple of variations on this "taking space."

MUTUALLY AGREED HIATUS

High-stakes relationships are the most likely candidates for a mutually agreed break. By "high-stakes relationships," I mean those that will have a lasting impact on your daily life if the relationship is severed; marriages and business partnerships are the obvious examples.

This break may be a physical separation—including cutting off other forms of direct communication—but it is far more likely that it will simply be a negotiated redrawing of the boundaries of the relationship, with a clearly understood moratorium on discussion of the incident with each other.

Under these circumstances, I would strongly recommend that each party individually make use of professional counseling during the agreed hiatus. And then make use of a trained mediator to facilitate the conversation between you.

It can be very tempting under such circumstances to make use of friends to play the role of mediator. This almost always ends badly. It is vital that the mediator have no vested interest in the outcome of the conversation and is seen by both individuals as being neutral. The role of the mediator here is to help both parties listen to each other effectively and to speak as honestly as possible. When the problems involved are deeply personal, it is also helpful if the mediator can be someone you are unlikely to ever encounter in any social setting.

You might find yourself wanting a space outside of formal counseling or mediation where you can talk through what is going on. In this case it may be helpful to speak to a friend, but make sure that this person can hold this space for you. By this I mean that the confidant will not speak about this beyond conversation with you, and that he or she can hold in respect the person with whom you are in conflict.

ONE PERSON STEPPING BACK

One person may require more time than the other to explore and investigate the new space in which they find themselves. There are two possible reasons why one person might need to step back for a while.

The wounding may have triggered a fault line for the one who has been wounded. If this is you, and you are able to see this, you may need to time to work out what has happened inside you, and to explore the deeper issues without fear of retriggering. It is best to communicate this to the one who has made the apology. Make no promises about future interaction; just ask to be allowed privacy while you do some self-exploration. Again I would strongly recommend some kind of professional help.

Attention shifts to the one who has apologized. In some cases it may be that the one who was wounded starts lashing out at you. Allow a little time for reasonable expression of anger, but if the behavior continues in spite of repeated genuine apology, it may be best to respectfully ask to cease contact for a period.

RE-ENGAGING

It is important that both parties respect the request for space. In such cases it is likely that contact won't be completely severed. Make sure that all conversations respect the boundary around the issue that has caused conflict. If you can make an appointment to re-engage, that is probably the best course. However, it may be that you find yourself veering, despite all your resolutions, into the "forbidden" conversation space. If that is the case, then one of you should make explicit what is happening. As you soon as you notice that you are discussing the issue, ask whether the other person is happy to pursue the conversation and ask you yourself whether you are prepared for the discussion. If not, close the conversation and shift back onto safer territory.

GIVE IT TIME!

It may take several attempts at engaging and needing space before you are both able to commit to reconciliation. In the interim, do the work you need to do. It is almost certain that, on whichever side of the conflict you are sitting, you will need to let go of your initial version of what happened. You need to be willing for your perspective to change. To that end, praying for patience and the graces of wisdom and empathy will help.

Remember that we humans are complex creatures. In any significant conflict, the matter is hardly ever the only thing going on in both people's lives. There are often other stressors that escalate the problem. Giving time can allow for the background stress to level out, which can in itself supply perspective.

Take some time to recall an incident where taking time proved useful in resolving a conflict. What shifted in you over time?

FOR THE ONE WHO HAS BEEN WOUNDED...

The key question to ask yourself at this time is whether this incident is the only one affecting you or whether something deeper is at play. Is there some other unresolved fear in you that is active? Are you transferring elements of an older relationship onto this person and their actions?

Bear in mind that most of us carry old wounds; and most of us do so unconsciously. We carry our baggage into new relationships, and this will have to be processed sooner or later. If you find the right people to help you deal with your wounding, tremendous healing can take place. This will begin to reduce the burden of emotional baggage that you carry. Remember, the fact that there is conflict and pain doesn't mean that the relationship itself is fundamentally flawed!

FOR THE FORGIVENESS COMPANION...

Your greatest challenge here will be patience. It can take a great deal of time to work through significant problems. There may be many false starts. Your job is to continue to support. With each false start, the wounded one will need time to get back onto solid ground. *Do not ask whether the person is still willing to remain in the relationship until they have found their internal equilibrium again.* A decision made in the smarting pain of a false start is unlikely to be a good one.

FOR THE ONE WHO DID THE WOUNDING...

The most important thing to remember here is that a new equilibrium needs to be found. If the relationship is to survive in the long term, you need to know what was triggered in the other. You also need to know what it was in yourself that precipitated the action that was perceived as a slight.

If this relationship is worth the long-term effort to you, it is worthwhile finding a way to be as generous as you can to the one who was wounded. Remember that it is almost inevitable that a time will come when the shoe will be on the other foot. While it may seem hard for you, it is well worth the investment in time and energy to give the relationship a real chance.

12

WHEN YOU CAN'T WALK AWAY

The greatest challenge of all lies in those situations in which true reconciliation is simply not available and walking away does not appear to be a viable option, either. The most common place for this challenge is in families, but it can also occur in the workplace. Reconciliation requires that both parties are willing to do the interior work required to access the apology or the forgiveness. Whichever side of the line you are currently standing on, it requires compassion. You have to be willing to put yourself in the shoes of the other—to accept that they are human too, that they (and you) can be irrationally hurt by minor slights, and that they (and you) can do things which are less than generous.

It requires a commitment to honesty and to humility. It requires that you allow yourself to see the other as a flawed human being—like you.

Unfortunately it is fairly common for one of the parties involved to be unwilling to take that journey of self-exploration, or even to be incapable of doing so. They want to hold to the role of victim or of the one who has been misunderstood.

They want to avoid taking responsibility for the hurtful interaction.

That desire and resistance is hardly ever conscious. But it is real, and it is an insurmountable barrier to true reconciliation.

The common approach these days is to say that you should cut people out of your life if you cannot enjoy a reasonably smooth interaction with them. The truth is that while people may make that choice in the case of friends, it is far, far harder to do so in families, as well as in some working situations.

Every family has a complex web of relationships, which may be dysfunctional to a greater or lesser degree. It can be very hard to admit to the world that there is any dysfunction within your family. For some, this is a silent shame. Most of us have had the experience of showing up at a family function and having to be painfully polite. There can, though, be serious issues, and sometimes none of us feels comfortable about broaching them. But the problems lurch into our consciousness when we see each other.

Oftentimes minor issues can be forgotten with time, if we all just keep showing up and doing the right thing. In time, new challenges can emerge that may realign allegiances in a healthier way. However, there are some incidents that are really hard to get over.

Some years ago, the father of a friend of mine died. It was clear for several weeks beforehand that the end was imminent. My friend's wife was not happy to have to her husband disappear across the country to be with his family of origin, and so he did not go until after his father had actually died. My friend's mother took this as a betrayal. She felt that she needed her son during those last, difficult days. After the funeral, harsh words were exchanged between my friend's mother and wife. Today, several years later, the tension remains. Both are strong women; both view their positions as justified, and neither will back down. As a result, their family gatherings continue to be painful for everyone.

The greatest challenge in family relationships seems to be the presumption that we can expect certain kinds of support from one another. That if the other doesn't show up for us in the way we feel he or she ought to, then we have a right to be angry or offended. The truth is that life is long and our capacity to show up for one another changes with time and with life circumstances. Our families of origin are not chosen; one can't always show up according to someone else's perceived need. We all have to find a way to drop our expectations of who the others should be for us.

That may sound very negative, but if other people persistently fail to show up in the way that you expect them to, maybe it is time to accept that they are simply who they are. If you can let go of our own expectations of what you need, you may be able to begin to see the gifts that they do genuinely have—and to appreciate them for who they are with all their limitations. This is true for all sorts of relationships that may go beyond family.

This is not easy, and I have certainly not perfected it. In fact, I would go so far as to say that I am still trying to figure out how to make it work. And failing a lot. But the intention feels good. If you can allow an offended person to simply be who he or she is, then maybe, just maybe, you can learn to coexist in a manner that isn't consistently hurtful to both of you.

It's worth remembering that in any relationship, we will encounter difficulties, and hurtful incidents may occur. Brené Brown makes the point in *Rising Strong* that trust and connection are possible in a relationship only where hurtful action is the exception. To take this further: this means that in a situation where the hurtful incident is part of the habitual way of relating, it is not reasonable for the "victim" to continue to put themselves in harm's way. This is the co-dependence of abuse. It is vitally important that you understand what it is you are trying to do if you are involved in such a scenario: you are trying to keep a civil relationship, but real connection will probably be way off the table.

Keeping a safe distance from someone who is abusive, even mildly so, and is still in your life is extremely difficult to do. It requires defining strong boundaries. You will also need to remind yourself of your commitment to an amicable, limited interaction each time you are part of a "problematic" gathering. It also requires that you continue to pray for the grace of forgiveness and interior freedom. But don't be fooled into thinking that this person is somehow "safe" for you to be around even though you've managed to forgive them and have attained some interior freedom.

There is no doubt that this path is the most challenging one. The probability of further wounding is high. You cannot keep trying to relate in the same way as before and hope that things will go well. You need to take time to rethink your strategy of relating. It may take several attempts and a good deal of time before you are able to find a new equilibrium. Bear in mind, too, that even if the other person is unwilling to have an honest conversation about a hurtful interaction—or is perhaps incapable of doing so— they are unlikely to be completely unaware of the problem. As a result, their responses toward you are likely to be strained.

Families carry huge amounts of "history," and in many cases there is not a clear victim and a clear perpetrator. Everyone will be vying for the victim spot. So it is worthwhile recalling frequently, as you commit and recommit to this process, that it is likely that everyone sees himself or herself as the wounded party, which means that in someone's eyes, you are the villain. And in truth, it is quite possible that you have indeed caused pain for the person who has wounded you.

Any complex system will resist change. Families are large systems and, as a result, changing the dynamic of how you relate to one another is intensely challenging. It will require persistent, conscious effort on your part to change the way in which you approach the problematic situation, and this will need to be repeated multiple times before the rest of the family can begin to settle into the new normal.

The period after there has been conflict is likely to be painful, frustrating, and fraught at times. But if you all really do want to have some kind of amicable relationship where you can gather happily for family occasions or holidays, the only option is to persist with as much openness and generosity of spirit as you can muster. But take care, all the same, to protect your own vulnerability.

The most effective way of recovering an amicable relationship is a commitment to kind action. Whenever there is an opportunity to do something that is kind or generous for the other—do it. Over time, this kind action will be the new normal that others expect from you. As their experience of who you are shifts to seeing you as someone who will step up and do kind and generous things, they will soften. This will make the arbitrary necessary conversation at a family gathering far more pleasant for both of you.

Just take care not to expect thanks for your actions!

It will be extremely tempting to think of yourself as taking the "higher road." Let that idea go; the spirit of that thought is one of superiority and will erode any efforts you are trying to make. Pray for the grace to accept the fact that you will probably not receive the apology that you think you are due. Pray for the grace of freedom from the desire for apology.

FOR THE ONE WHO HAS BEEN WOUNDED...

There is a real balance to be struck here. If there is emotional manipulation or subtle abuse in play, it may be almost impossible to walk this road. The reason for choosing this road is almost always because there are other people who could be adversely affected by your decision to sever the relationship completely. It is a tough path to walk, and it is probably helpful to revisit your choice from time to time to ascertain whether anything in the environment has shifted—either for better or for worse.

This path will require a conscious commitment to acting with kindness.

Situations in which you have continuing contact are probably the most challenging in which to actually achieve forgiveness, because the behavior of the other may not change at all. If your actions are founded on an expectation that they will bring about change, you are likely to be disappointed. Your actions must be based in your own motivation to do the right thing for the greater good of the community.

FOR THE FORGIVENESS COMPANION...

The one who was wounded will likely need a space to unload disappointment at the lack of change. Over time, what the person needs from having space may slowly change, and it is helpful if you are able to point this out. Perhaps more than once.

FOR THE ONE WHO DID THE WOUNDING...

If you are aware that you have caused pain for a member of your community and that person has chosen to step back a little from the intimacy you once enjoyed, it is worthwhile trying to ask what he or she thinks has happened. The complexity here is almost always that who is wounded and who did the wounding may not be clear cut. You may have your own pain. It is best for you to try and act with as much kindness and generosity as you can. If a conversation is either not possible or not desirable for one of you, respect that. Do the best that you can to maintain a civil relationship.

13

OLD WOUNDS RESURFACING

So far, most of what I have written has been targeted at resolving relatively fresh wounds. But all of us carry the scars of woundings that have been around for a long, long time. I think most of us would like to be free of those woundings. And it is quite likely that the woundings that we struggle with today have tendrils in our past.

There is a popular train of thought that appears quite attractive: simply forget about the past and focus on the blessings of today. The problem is, those pesky past woundings don't go away with that strategy. The focus on the blessings of today turns out to be numbing behavior, not real healing. I have found that finally managing to let go of the high school wounding has enabled me to explore the early childhood wounding. I was aware of the early childhood stuff for a good six or seven years prior to letting go of the high school incident. But once that space opened up in my psyche, I found I had new access to the earlier wounding. As a result, I have had to spend some time simply owning my version of my early experience. It has been painful to sit with some of the wounds that I carry, and to recognize the ways in which they have unconsciously shaped all of my interactions.

I should add here that, often, childhood wounding is not caused by any deliberate or intentional action of others. Unless there has been specific abuse, it is usually simply the product of trying to survive in a system that is at least to some degree dysfunctional.

Those past woundings will continue to trip us up if we do not address them. I had a powerful realization some months ago: I know that I withdraw when I don't feel safe, but I hadn't realized the extent to which I was unconsciously operating through that mechanism. A brief conversation with one of my closest friends, in which she made a comment which left me feeling profoundly isolated, triggered this unconscious withdrawal reflex. Had it not been for her persistence in asking me what was wrong, we would have gradually drifted apart.

That mechanism was rooted in my early childhood wounding and, despite the fact that I am a person who reflects deeply on life, I was completely unaware of its operation. I knew I had easily walked away from situations before, and I knew I had allowed a close friendship with another colleague to fade, but I didn't understand at all that this withdrawal reaction was in play. Now that I know it is there, I am far more able to moderate my own response. Now, I am capable of returning to the person who has inadvertently triggered my defensive survival mechanism and having a conversation about what happened. In some cases, walking away will still be the appropriate response, but now I can actively choose!

When old wounds reappear there can be a sense of frustration or shame: "This old thing again?!" The only way to deal with these productively is to haul them out into the light and look them square in the eye. In such a case, it is probably important to find a forgiveness companion. Indeed, it may be useful to find professional help. Your habitual way of looking at what happened will make it very difficult to reframe the situation for yourself. Talk it through with someone, and follow the pattern outlined above for a fresher wound. Look for the perspective you may not have seen before; look for the humanity of the others involved; look for the areas in which you may not have been entirely innocent.

There are two important considerations with old wounds. All of us carry some degree of childhood wounding because parents are also wounded people. Despite the best intentions, with the stresses of having a young family, things go wrong—and children pick up messages that shape their world view. An active forgiveness process that entails having conversations with those who caused the childhood wounding may not be helpful. In families, we are exposed to the best and the worst of one another. As a child, you start to internalize messages about the relative safety of the world, and your sense of how you belong in the world begins to develop before you even have words. Oftentimes a particular worldview is unconsciously handed on from generation to generation.

The second consideration is that the people beyond your family who hurt you a long time ago are probably not the same people today. They, too, have had years of living and growing. Under the same circumstances, they might well choose different actions today. They are frozen in your mind as "hurtful" because of a particular incident, but there is almost certainly more to them than this.

I would strongly recommend spending some time considering whether you have old wounds to forgive or let go of. Don't worry if you are slightly embarrassed that you are still holding onto things that seem small, things which happened years or decades ago. Open yourself to the possibility of learning something. I guarantee that if you take the journey, you will find an increase in interior freedom.

Remember that you can't will yourself to let go or to forgive. Just keep praying for the grace.

EPILOGUE

It has been my experience that forgiveness is a vital component of interior freedom. It isn't the only factor, but interior freedom is not possible in the absence of forgiveness. As both compassion and real connection with others seem to be inextricably linked to interior freedom, forgiveness is essential.

Forgiveness doesn't happen magically with time. I am not referring to the small woundings that happen every day and that we happily shake off. Think of the things you have found truly galling; the events which have changed the way you look at and relate to the person who has wounded you. Those life-shaping events don't just resolve themselves; *you have to actively forgive.*

And if you are the one who caused pain (even if utterly unintentionally), *it is right to apologize.*

The impact of any event is entirely personal and will be related to your own history and your own worldview. Things that shake you to the core may be hardly noticed by someone else. You have to be true to your own experience. Don't try and rationalize your way out of feeling the way you do. Allow yourself to feel the hurt; then ask yourself why you are experiencing this particular event to be so painful.

Talking about forgiveness and the events that have caused you pain requires you to be vulnerable. Make sure that the person you are opening up to has the capacity both to respect you and to hold you. Not all people have this capacity.

Forgiveness does mean letting go. And a result, there may be an element of grief over what has happened. Give yourself the time you need to grieve what has been lost.

Jonathan Sacks, commenting on resolving conflict between siblings, writes: "The past does not dictate the future. To the contrary, a future of reconciliation can, in some measure at least, retroactively redeem the past."[21]

It is my firm belief that this new future and redemption of the past is possible through the grace of forgiveness—whether reconciliation is possible or not. But there are no shortcuts! You cannot bypass the experience of the pain, the anger, the grief. It is only when you allow yourself to risk being overwhelmed by your emotion, risk facing into the potential loss of relationships that were once precious to you, and daring to pray for the grace of forgiveness, that this new hope and recovery of the past is made possible.

Ultimately though, it is well worth the investment of time and psycho-spiritual energy. If you carry your emotional baggage in your body, you will, in time, notice a physical shift. You will feel the change in the very depths of your being.

---

21   Jonathan Sacks, *Not in God's Name* (New York: Schocken Books, 2015), p. 158.